BOOK #10 "ROLL FOR

TUTTLE TWINS • BOOK #10 • First Printing Nov 2022
Published by: **Tuttle Twins Show, llc** © 2022, all rights reserved
Printed by: **Shyft Global**

Showrunner: **Daniel Harmon** Director: **Tyler Stevens**
Writers: **Jonny Vance, Daniel Harmon, Zach Atherton, Jessica Rigby**

Graphic Novel Art Director: **Jared Sampson**
Interior Layouts, Design, FX, and Lettering by:
Ben Woolston, Jay Layne, Brooke Hancock, Jonathan Castro, Kenyon Davis, J. James McFarland
Front Cover Design: **Scott Brooks**
Editor: **Becky Ross Michael**

All artistic representations of prominent characters featured herein and all likenesses are trademarks of Tuttle Twins Show, LLC unless otherwise noted. No part of this publication may be reproduced or transmitted in any form or by any means without the express written permission of Tuttle Twins Show, LLC. This print media is a reproduction and interpretation of the tv series "TUTTLE TWINS" and falls under appropriate copyrights to the intellectual properties of all parties involved. All artwork created is officially licensed.
For more information please contact admin@tuttletwins.tv.

WWW.TUTTLETWINS.TV   **@TUTTLETWINSTV**

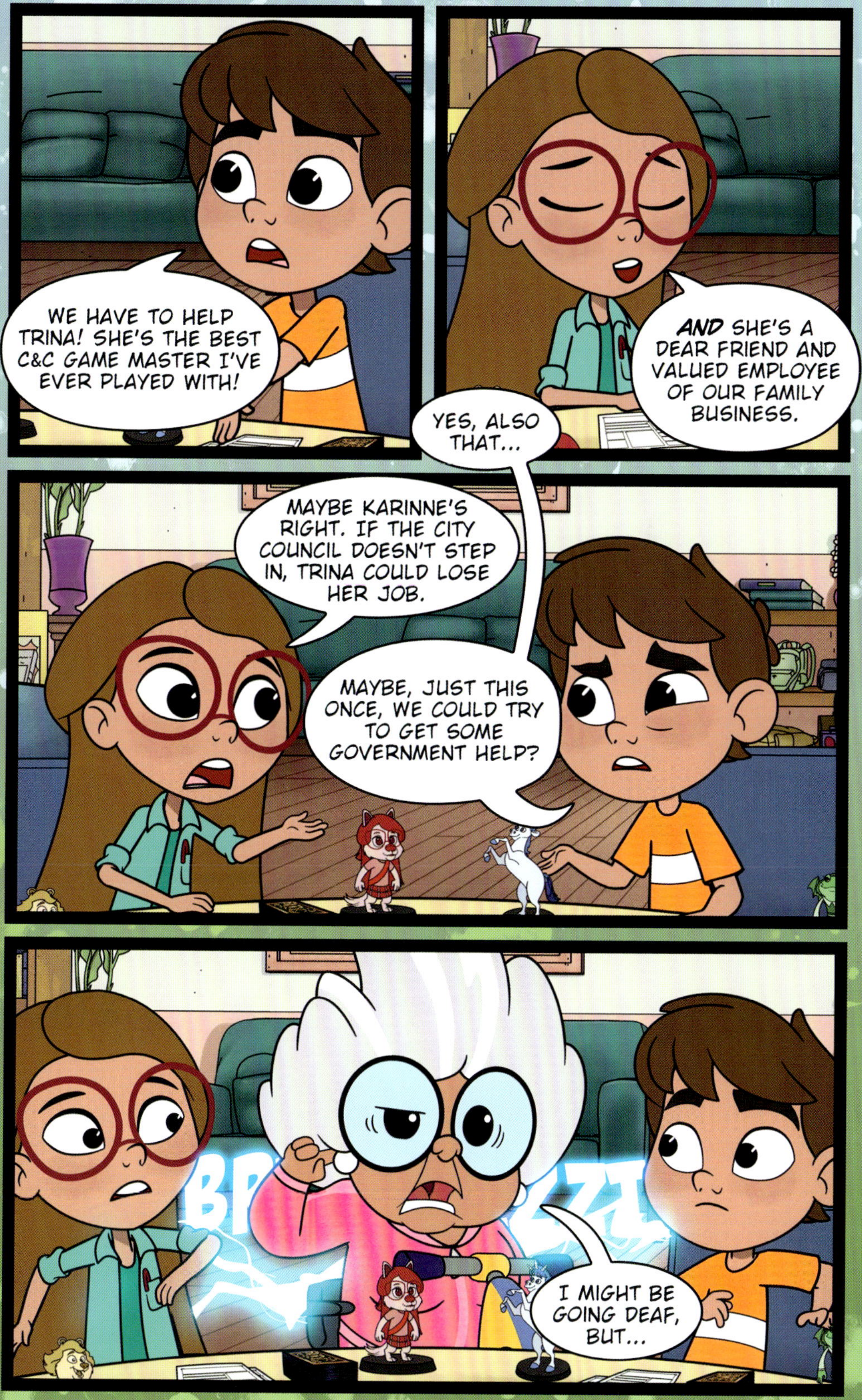

WASHINGTON D.C. 1926

THE PEOPLE DID. WE CUT TAXES AND SPENDING.
AND WITH MORE OF THEIR OWN MONEY IN THEIR POCKETS, PEOPLE REPAIRED THE ECONOMY THEMSELVES.
SCAMPER
SCAMPER
YOU DIDN'T HELP ANYONE OUT?!
IT WAS TEMPTING, TRUST ME. BUT THE GOVERNMENT'S LIKE A LEVIATHAN.
YOU PLAY C&C?!

HEAVENS NO! WHAT DO I LOOK LIKE, A ZOZZLED DEWDROPPER?!
I- NO!
HMMMM
EMILY... EMILY'S SO INTO THAT.

WHAT I MEAN IS, THE GOVERNMENT'S LIKE A LEVIATHAN MONSTER THAT GROWS TO UNSTOPPABLE SIZE.
$ = 1 CUP OF MILK
ONE, PLEASE.
BUT WHAT IF YOU GROW THE GOVERNMENT TO DO SOMETHING GOOD, LIKE HELP A FRIEND?
SLASH A REALLY GOOD C&C MASTER?

ORDER'S UP!

CLINK!

JUMP

IF YOU WANT THE GOVERNMENT TO SOLVE YOUR PROBLEMS, YOU HAVE TO SURRENDER YOUR OWN POWER.

AND WHEN YOU DO, THAT POWER IS VERY HARD TO GET BACK.

GIVING INTO FEAR MAKES YOUR POWER DISAPPEAR.

GET BACK HERE, YA FILTHY RACCOONS!!
THAT'S WHY WE KEEP OUR GOVERNMENT SMALL.
EHH- THAT'S WHY WE USED TO DO THAT.
SQURIT!
COUGH
USED TO?!
COUGH

Panel 1: THIS IS SOUNDING A LOT LIKE THOSE SCARY SCI-FI BOOKS YOU LET ME BORROW.

THOSE ARE CALLED HISTORY BOOKS, CAL.

Panel 2: SQUIRT

Panel 3: KIPPERS KNICKERS! YOU MEAN ALL THE HORRORS ARE GOING TO HAPPEN?

YOU CURIOUS, CAL? WANNA SEE?
GASP!
FWIP
CLIMB
CLIMB
I USUALLY DON'T LIKE SPOILERS...

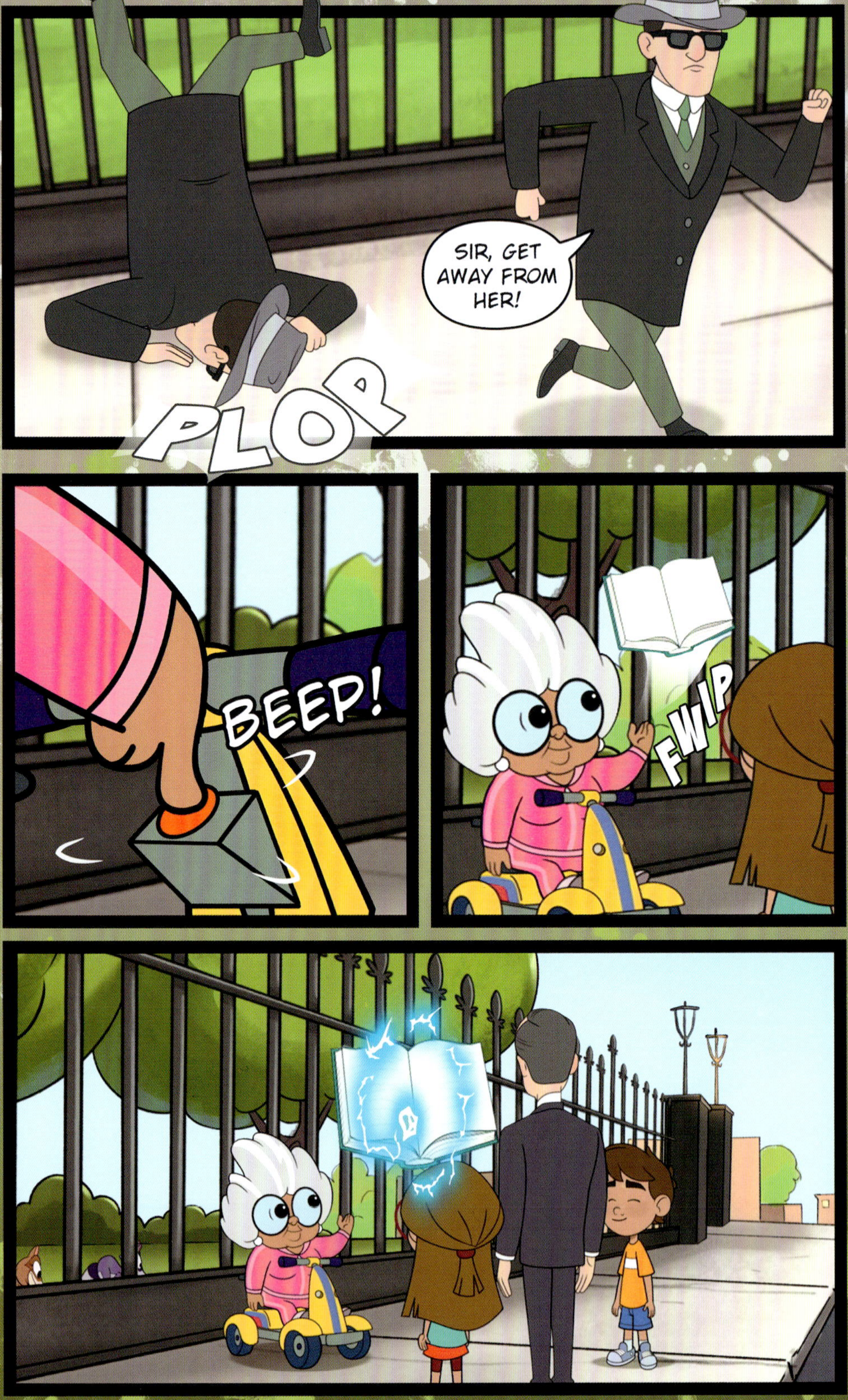
SIR, GET AWAY FROM HER!
PLOP
BEEP!
FWIP

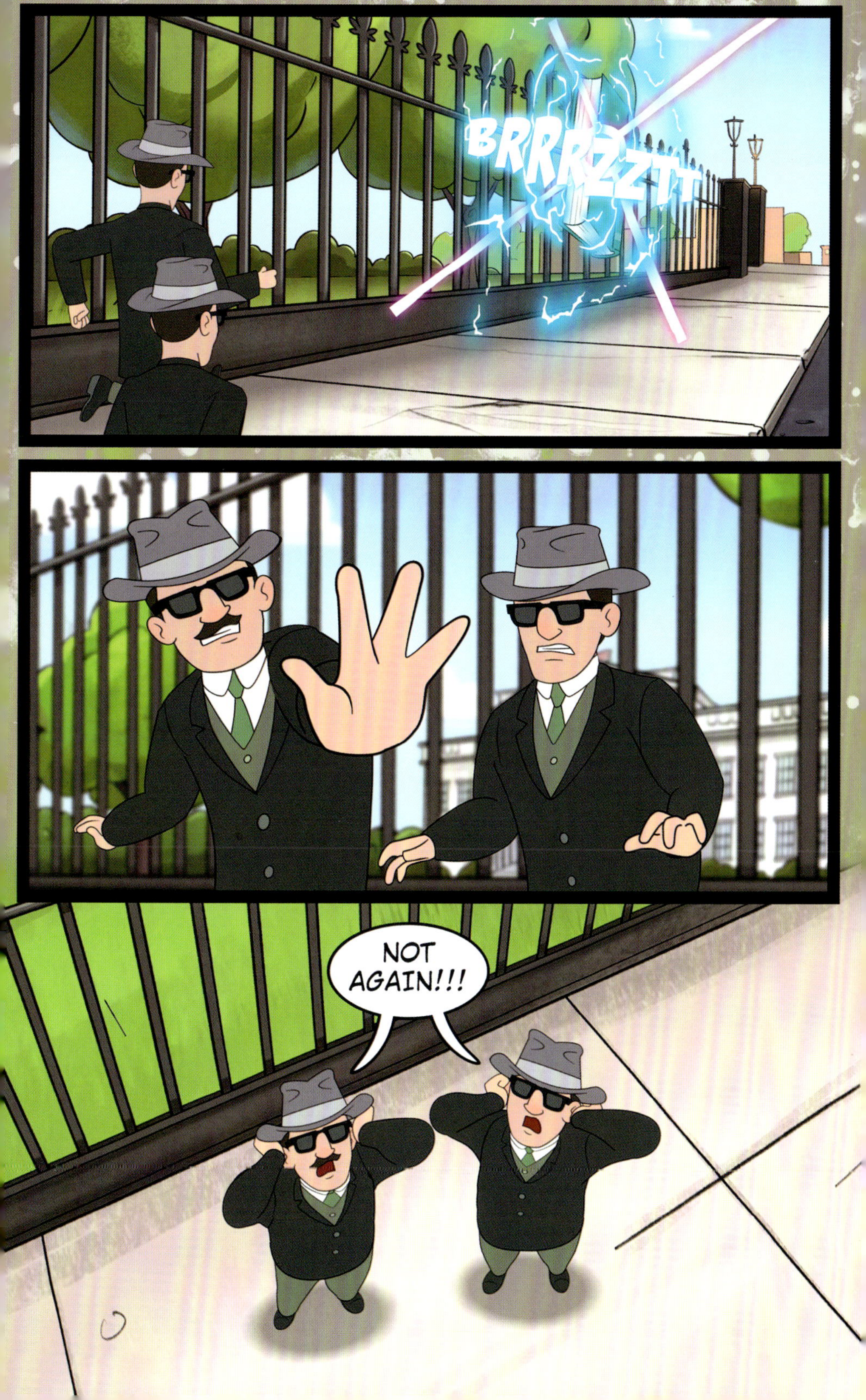
BRRRZZZTT
NOT AGAIN!!!

NEW YORK
WHAT IS THIS?
ACCORDING TO MY HORROR-
AHEM, ***HISTORY*** BOOK...
New York
1929
JUST 10 YEARS AFTER I LEFT OFFICE, THERE WAS ***ANOTHER*** RECESSION.

GASP!
GO ON...
I'M SORRY, I JUST READ AHEAD.
BUT THIS TIME, THE GOVERNMENT DECIDED TO STEP IN, INSTEAD OF LETTING THE COMMUNITIES HANDLE IT THEMSELVES.
IT'S TRUE! MANY SCHOLARS AGREE THAT THIS TURNED THE RECESSION INTO THE GREAT DEPRESSION.
RAW MILK
CLOSED

THAT *IS* DEPRESSING.
MILLIONS LOST THEIR JOBS AND HOMES.
CLOSED
$ = 1 CUP
PEOPLE WERE SCARED. SO THE GOVERNMENT TOOK MORE POWER AND CREATED SOMETHING CALLED ***THE NEW DEAL.***
STAMP
NEW DEAL

"THEY TOLD FARMERS HOW MUCH TO GROW, HOW MUCH THINGS SHOULD COST, AND HOW MUCH PEOPLE COULD BE PAID..."

REACHED GROWTH LIMIT!

"THEY EVEN BANNED PEOPLE FROM OWNING *GOLD!*"

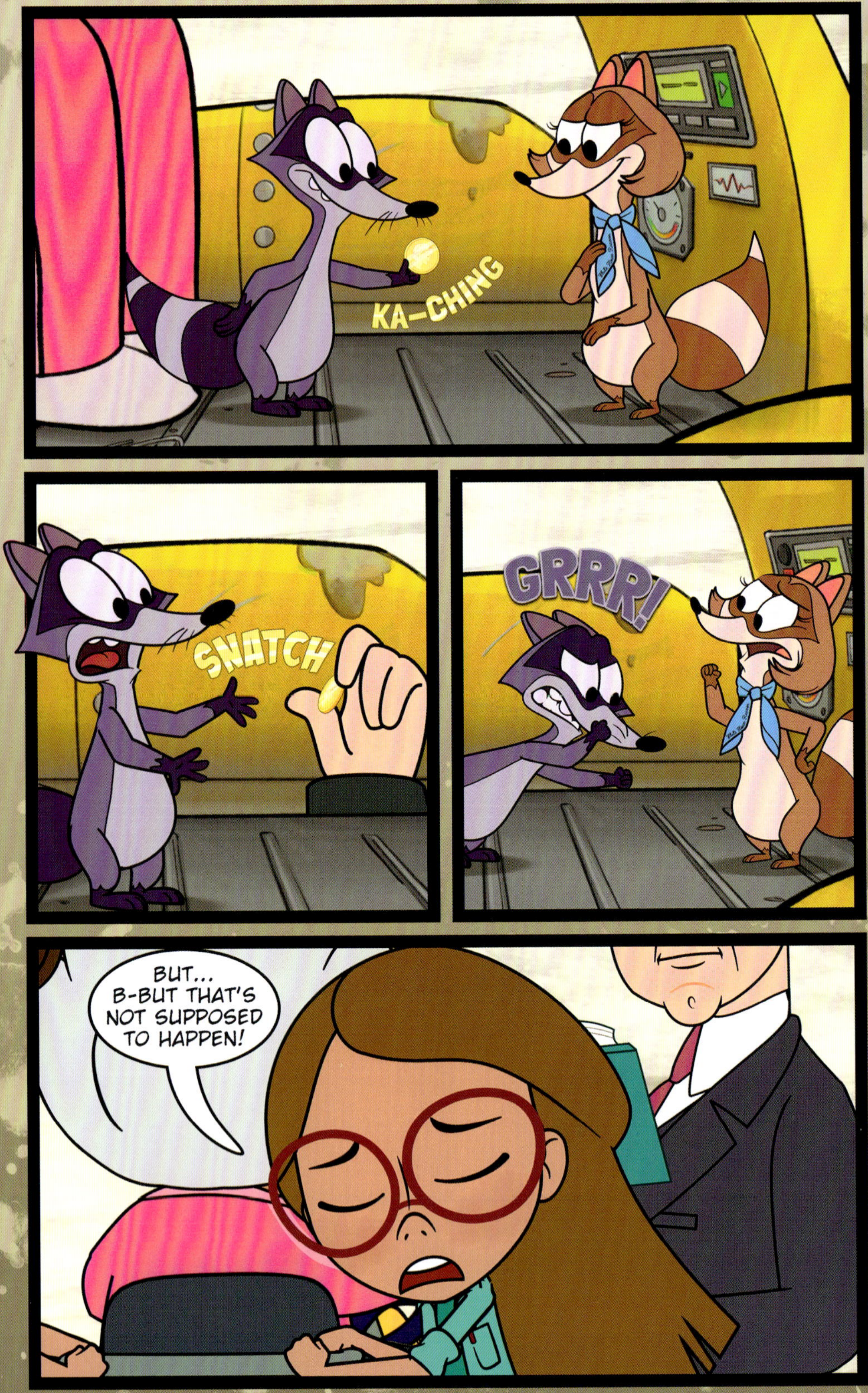
KA-CHING
SNATCH
GRRR!
BUT... B-BUT THAT'S NOT SUPPOSED TO HAPPEN!

NEITHER WAS THIS WEIRD MOLE.
THAT'S A RAISIN.
PLUCK
OHO, SCORE!
NOM!
EWW...
WAIT! BUT DOESN'T THE GOVERNMENT GIVE THE POWER BACK ONCE THE CRISIS IS OVER?
NO. THAT'S THE PROBLEM WITH THE LEVIATHAN.

WHOOOOSH

"THE MORE POWER YOU GIVE IT, THE MORE POWER IT KEEPS."

"THE LEVIATHAN GROWS BIGGER AND BIGGER WITH EACH CRISIS. AND IT'S NOT JUST THE ECONOMY EITHER."

WITH THE CRISIS OF WORLD WAR II, THE GOVERNMENT CREATED DOZENS OF NEW MILITARY PROGRAMS.

BUT AFTER THE WAR, THEY NEVER WENT AWAY...

...THEY JUST CHANGED NAMES, COSTING TAX PAYERS TRILLIONS.

BEWARE THE MILITARY INDUSTRIAL COMPLEX!
PRES. EISENHOWER
9/11 MEMORIAL
AFTER A TERRORIST ATTACK, THE GOVERNMENT TOOK OUR RIGHT TO PRIVACY.
NATIONAL
SECURITY

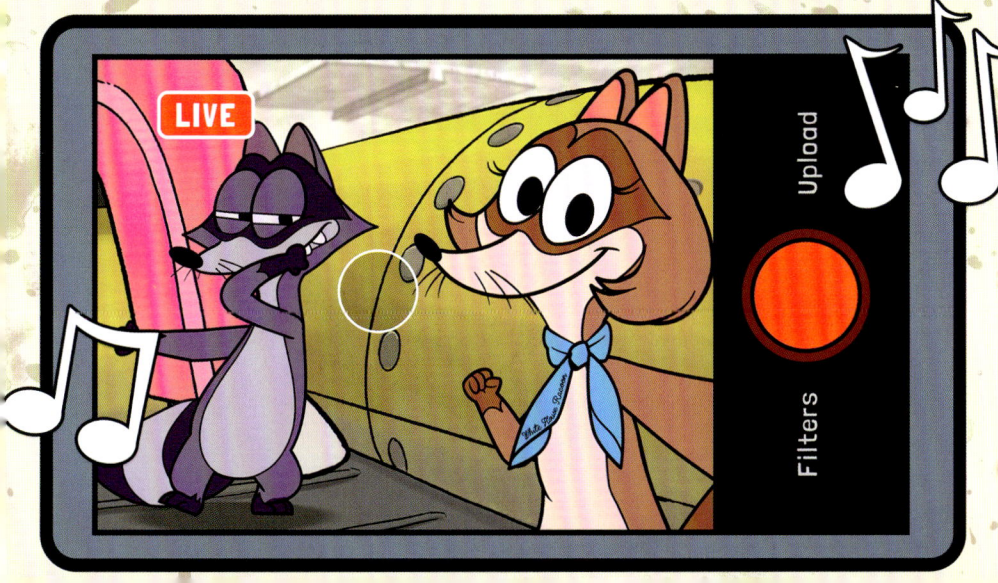

THEY DECLARED THEY COULD SPY ON US THROUGH OUR DEVICES.

BUT THEY JUST USE THIS DURING A CRISIS, RIGHT?

LIVE

Upload

Filters

OH NO. THEY'RE STILL DOING IT NOW.
EH?!
LIVE
Upload
Filters
NYAH!
Permanently Closed
Closed
Permanently Closed

AND DURING A VIRAL PANDEMIC, THE GOVERNMENT TOOK MANY OTHER FREEDOMS.

THEY TOLD CHURCHES THEY COULDN'T ASSEMBLE...

Stay Safe & God Bless

AND FORCED BUSINESSES TO CLOSE.

MANY NEVER REOPENED THEIR DOORS.

Permanently Closed

THE GOVERNMENT IN YOUR TIME IS OVER FIVE TIMES BIGGER THAN IT WAS WHEN I WAS YOUR AGE.

AND WITH EACH CRISIS, PEOPLE GET SCARED, SURRENDER THEIR FREEDOMS AND THE LEVIATHAN GROWS BIGGER.

RRAAAAH!!
CLOSED
R
$ = 1 CUP OF MILK
ISN'T THE GOVERNMENT SUPPOSED TO SERVE THE PEOPLE?
SURE. BUT A MONSTER THIS BIG DOESN'T HAVE TO SERVE YOU IF IT DOESN'T WANT TO.

I'M FEELING A LITTLE WOOZY.

PROBABLY THE RAW MILK.

BUT- GRANDMA! YOU SAID IT WAS SAFE.

I NEVER SAID IT WAS SAFE. FREEDOM HAS REAL RISKS.

BUT TRADING FREEDOM FOR SECURITY RARELY TURNS OUT HOW PEOPLE WANT.

BRRZZT

BRRZZT
RAW MILK
SO IF I'M HEARING YA, AND I THINK I AM- THE GOVERNMENT CAN'T DO ANY GOOD,
AND WE SHOULD OVERTHROW IT!

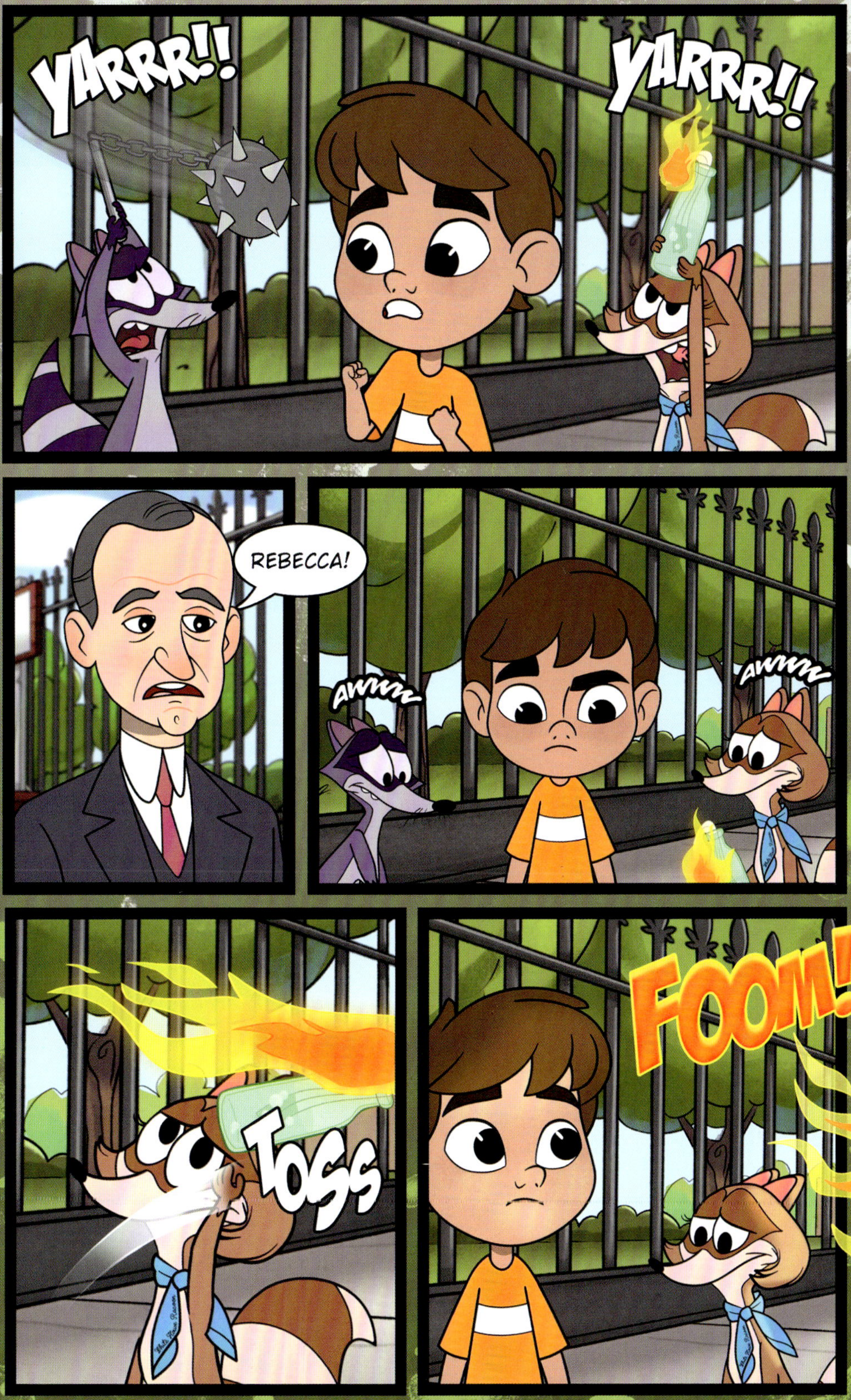
YARRR!!
YARRR!!
REBECCA!
AWWW
AWWW
TOSS
FOOM!

Panel 1: "I WOULDN'T BE PRESIDING OVER THE GOVERNMENT IF I THOUGHT THAT."

"THE GOVERNMENT CAN AND DOES DO GOOD, LIKE PROTECTING OUR RIGHTS. IT JUST NEEDS TO BE KEPT IN CHECK."

Panel 2: "SO HOW DO WE STOP THE LEVIATHAN FROM GROWING MORE?"

Panel 3: "GIVE PEOPLE THE TRUTH. AND LET THEM KEEP THE POWER TO SOLVE THEIR OWN PROBLEMS."

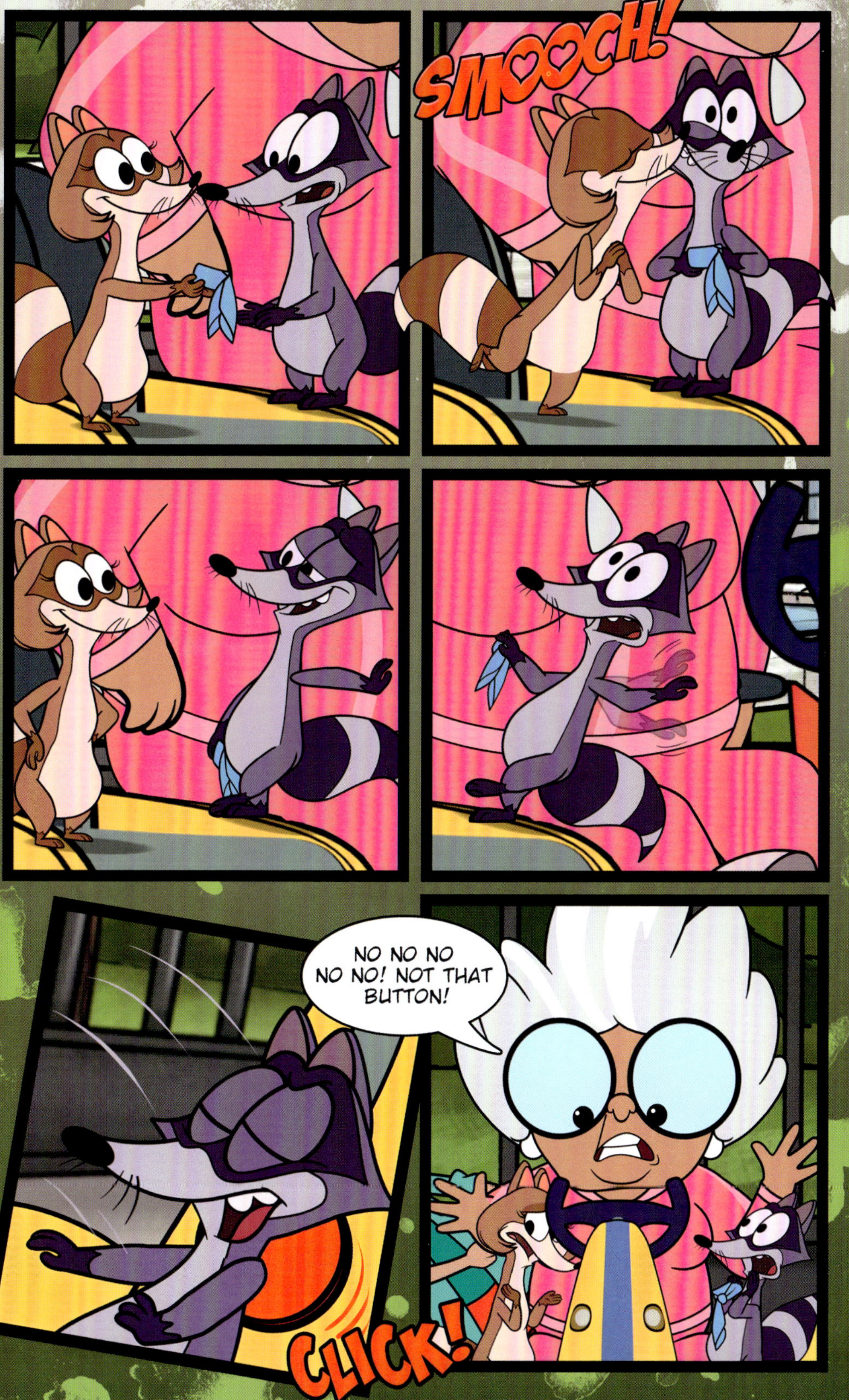
SMOOCH!
NO NO NO NO NO! NOT THAT BUTTON!
CLICK!

WHAT BUTTON??
THE IRONICALLY CONVENIENT PLOT TWIST BUTTON!
MEHREK!
REMEHKA!
BRRZZT

WHERE ARE WE?
AN EPIC FOREST?
A VILLAGE OF ANTHROPOMORPHIC SHEEP?

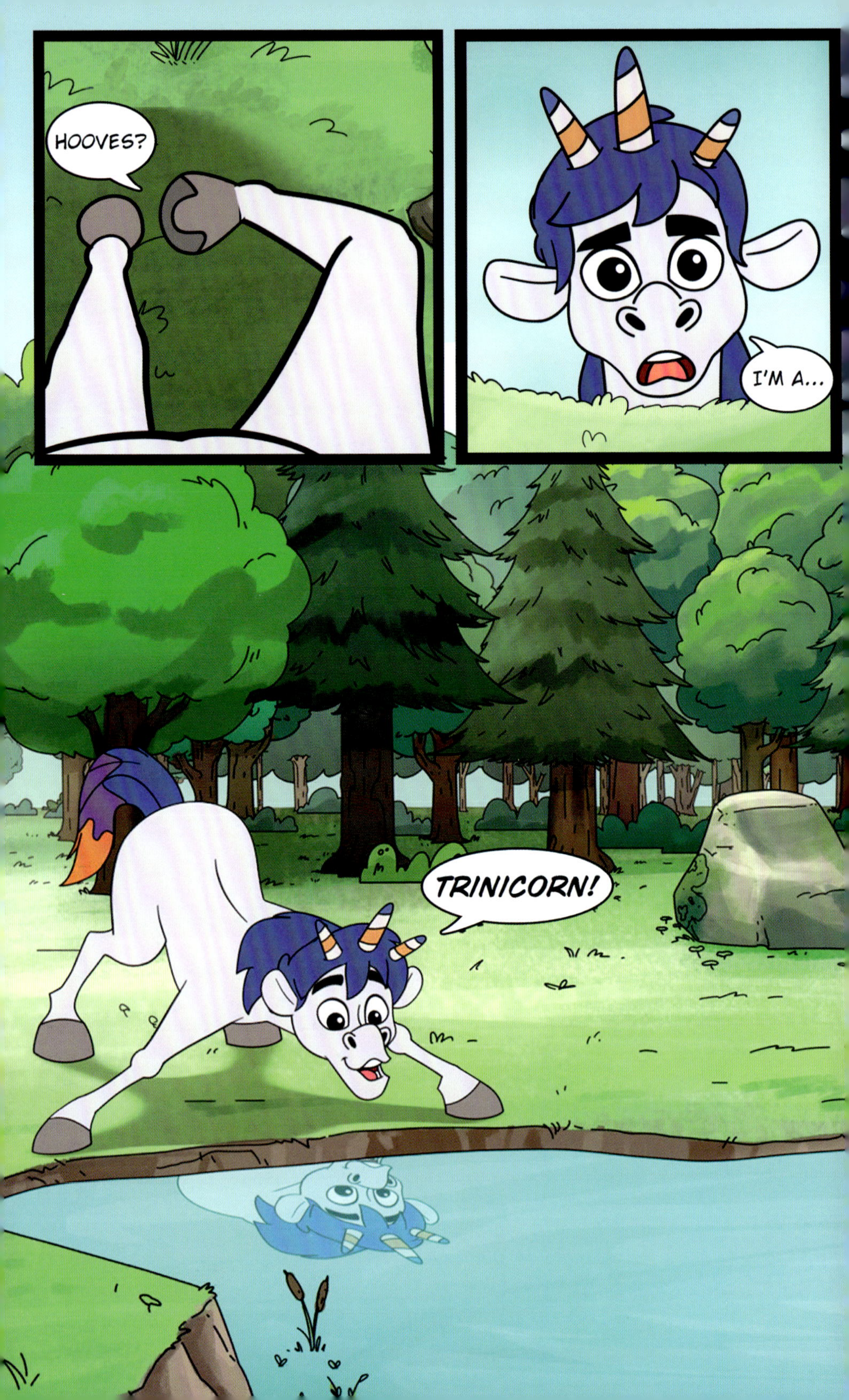
HOOVES?
I'M A...
TRINICORN!

GLITTER DANDRUFF?! DREAMS DO COME TRUE.
AND LOOK AT ME! I'M A WEREPUPPY!
HOOOOOOOW!

OH, NO! I'M NICE AND ADORABLE!

SEE?

B-AWWWWW!

EMILY! WE'RE IN THE GAME!

THIS IS AMAZ-

WHACK!!

RAWR

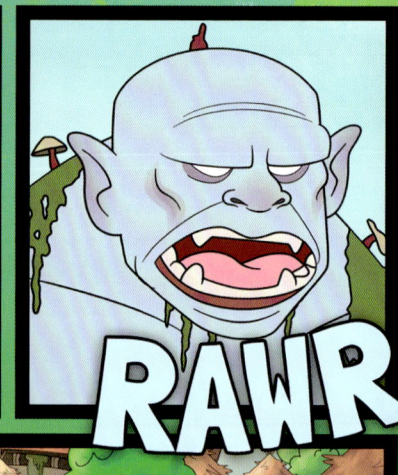

AHHHHH! AHHHHH!

RAAA!!!

ETHAN! ARE YOU OKAY!?

SMASH!

YEAH... HE ONLY HIT ONE OF MY STOMACHS. I STILL HAVE TWO LEFT.

POP!

POP!

TRINICORNS HAVE THREE OF EVERYTHING!

POP!

WE HAVE TO GET OUT OF HERE! GRANDMA!?
GRANDMA!
I REALLY NEED TO GET RID OF THAT BUTTON. AND DON'T WORRY, DEREK-

SIIIIGHHH...

THEY JUST HAVE TO LEARN ENOUGH TO FILL UP THE TANK.
E
F
THEN WE'LL HAVE ENOUGH KNOWLEDGE JUICE TO ZAP THEM BACK INTO THE REAL WORLD. PASS ME KARINNE'S DEMAFROG FIGURINE, I'D HATE FOR IT TO GET IN THE GAME.
DEREK!
PUSH

BZZT
DISCOUNTS!
OKAY! UH- MAYBE WORRY A LITTLE BIT.
WELCOME
BIENVENID
BIENVENUE
WELKOM
BEM-VINDO
VÄLKOMMEN
환영
NOM

SMASH

"WE HAVE TO SAVE THE VILLAGERS!"

"OK! AS LONG AS WE DON'T GIVE INTO FEAR, WE CAN FIGURE THIS OUT TOGETHER!"

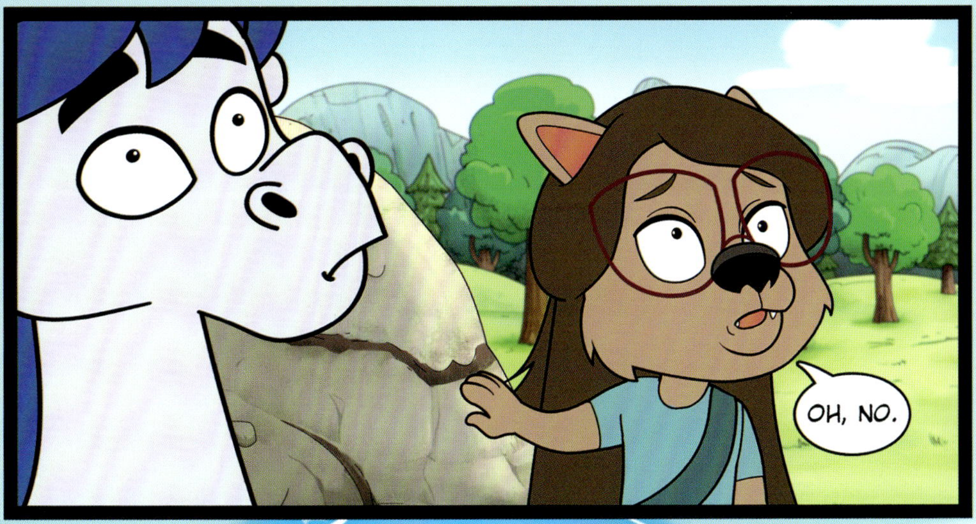
OH, NO.
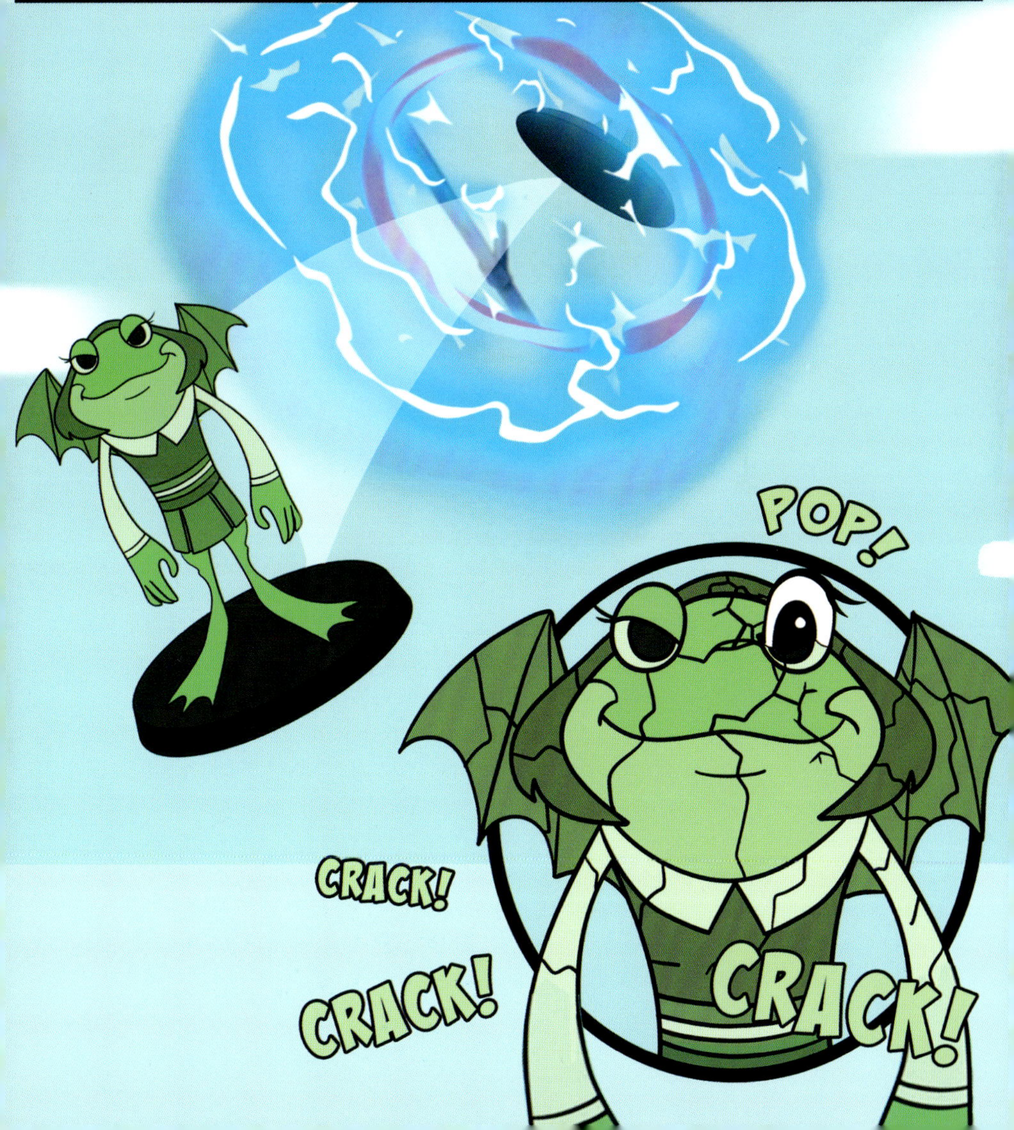
POP!
CRACK!
CRACK!
CRACK!

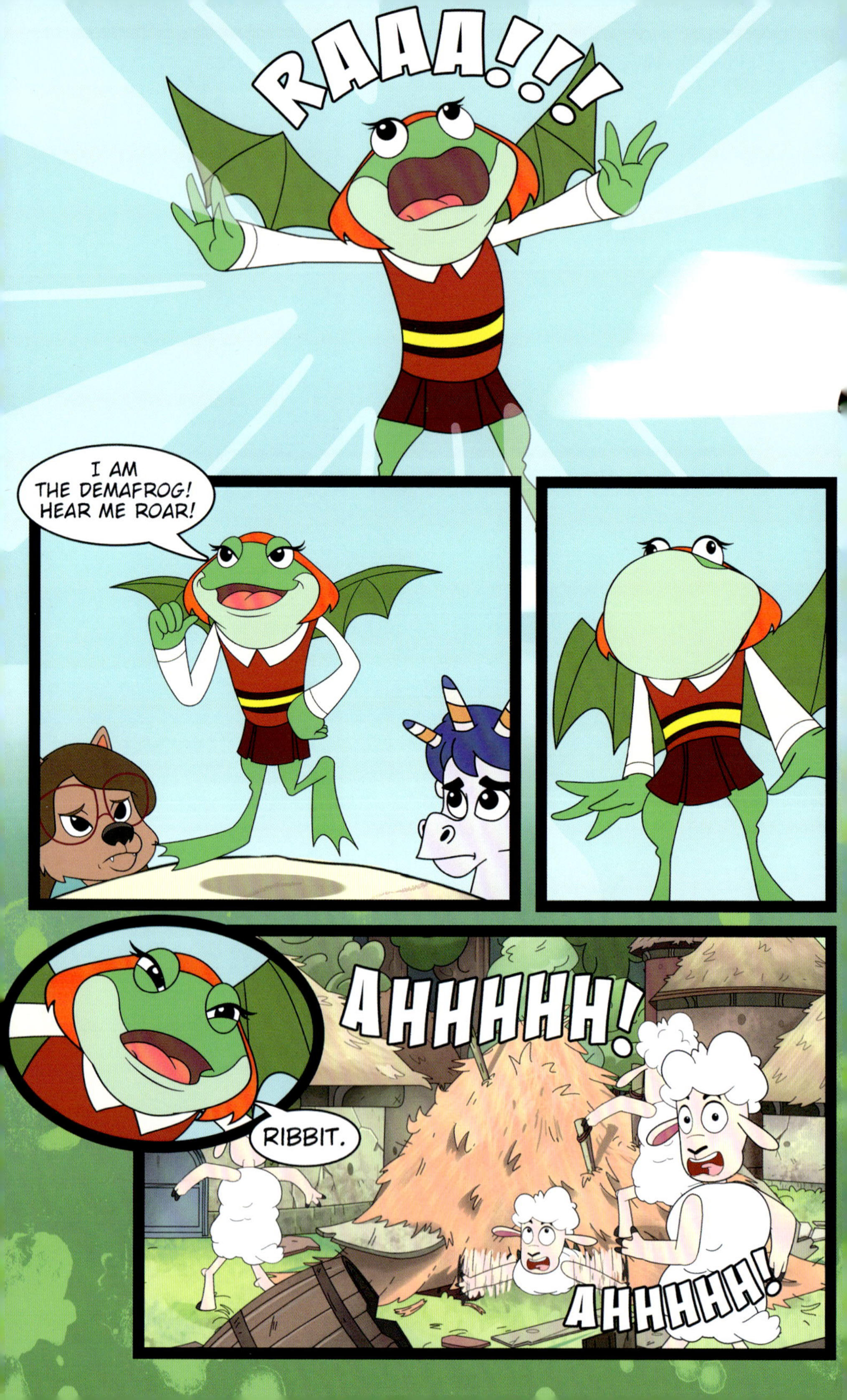
RAAA!!!
I AM THE DEMAFROG! HEAR ME ROAR!
AHHHHH!
RIBBIT.
AHHHHH!

SMASH!
IN A CRISIS, I SEE?
IT'S NOTHING A LITTLE LEVIATHAN CAN'T SOLVE!
SNAP!
COME HERE, LITTLE LEVI!
WHAT ARE YOU DOING UP THERE, LITTLE...

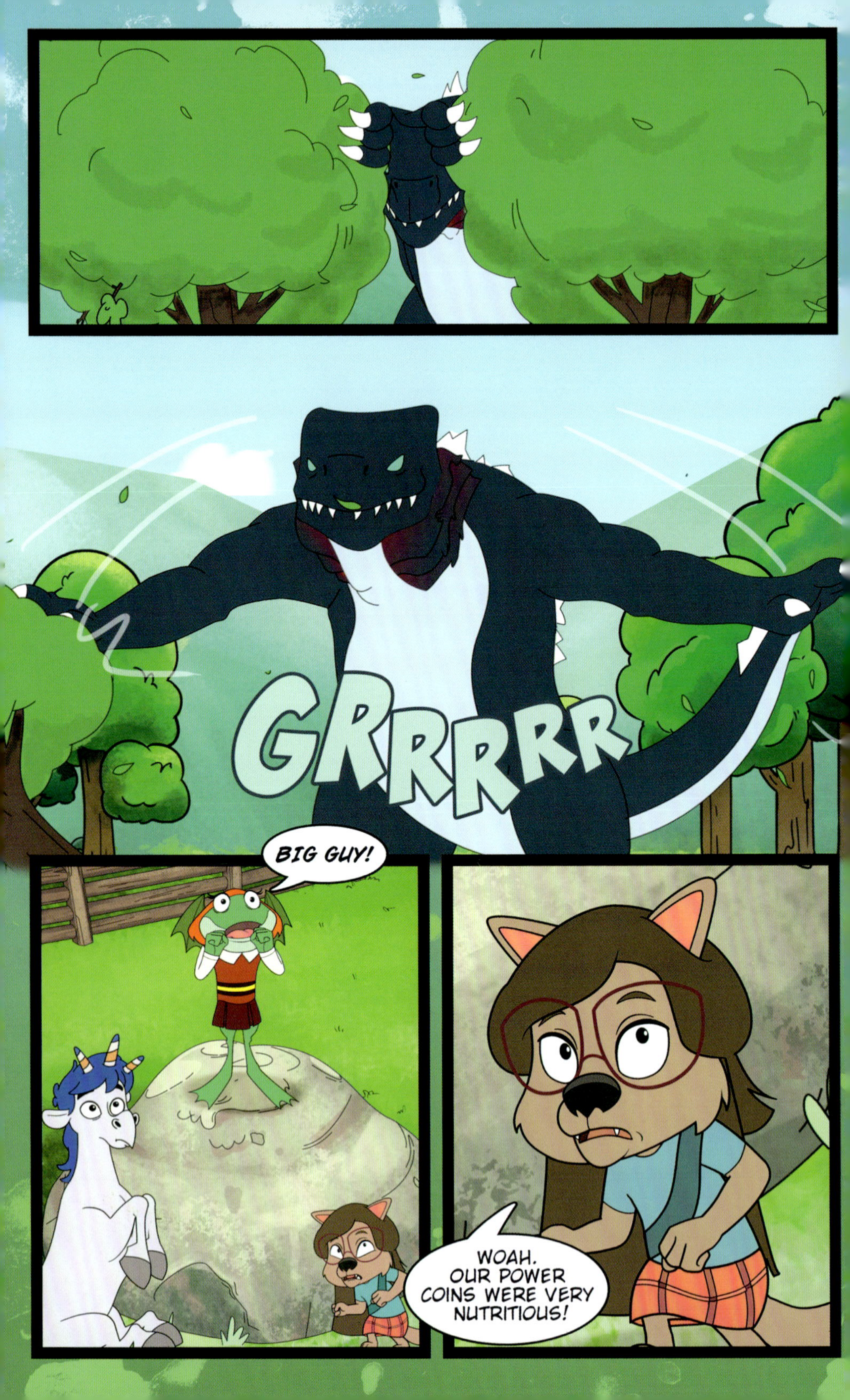
GRRRRR
BIG GUY!
WOAH.
OUR POWER
COINS WERE VERY
NUTRITIOUS!

FWIP

GRRRRR

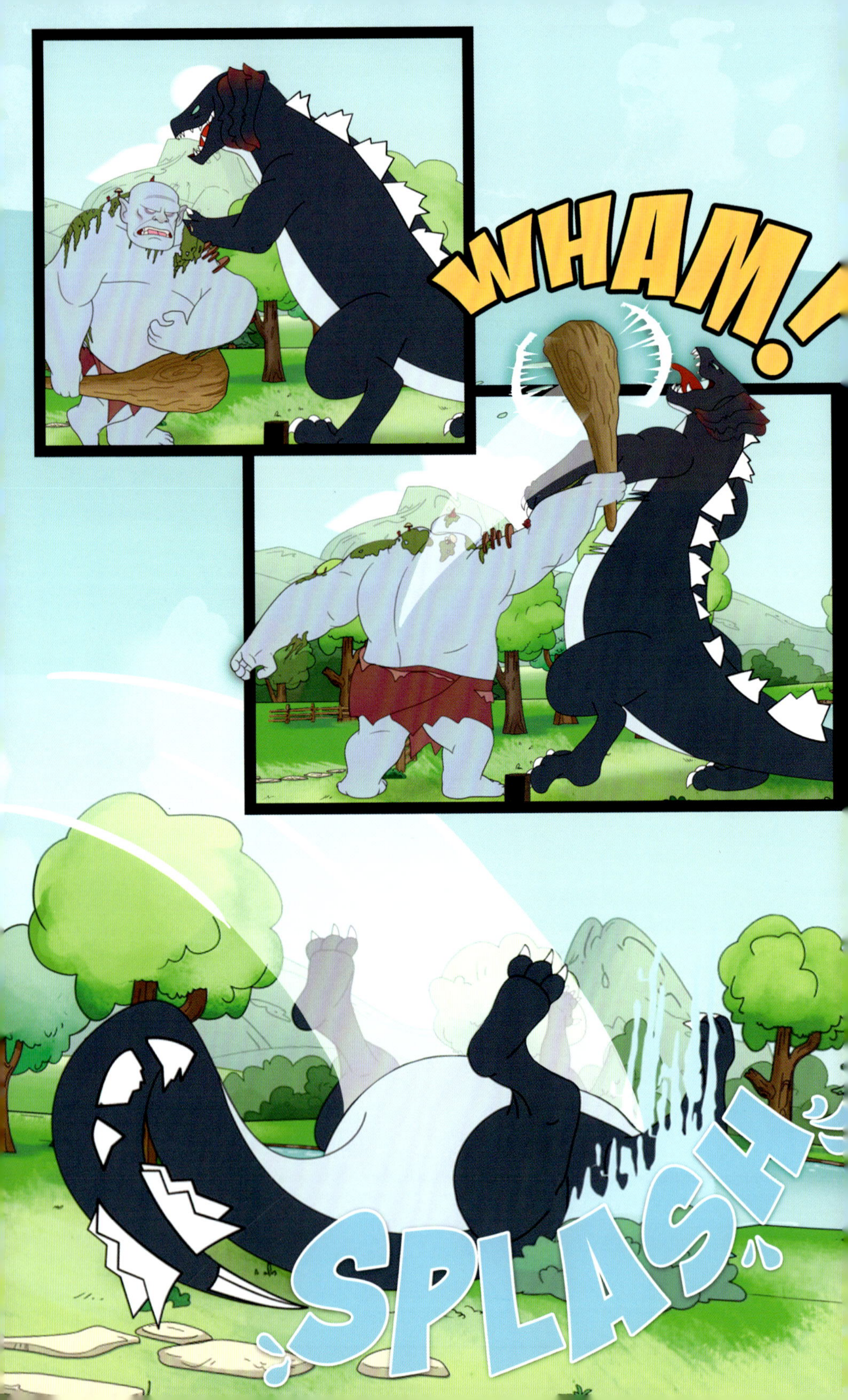
WHAM!
SPLASH

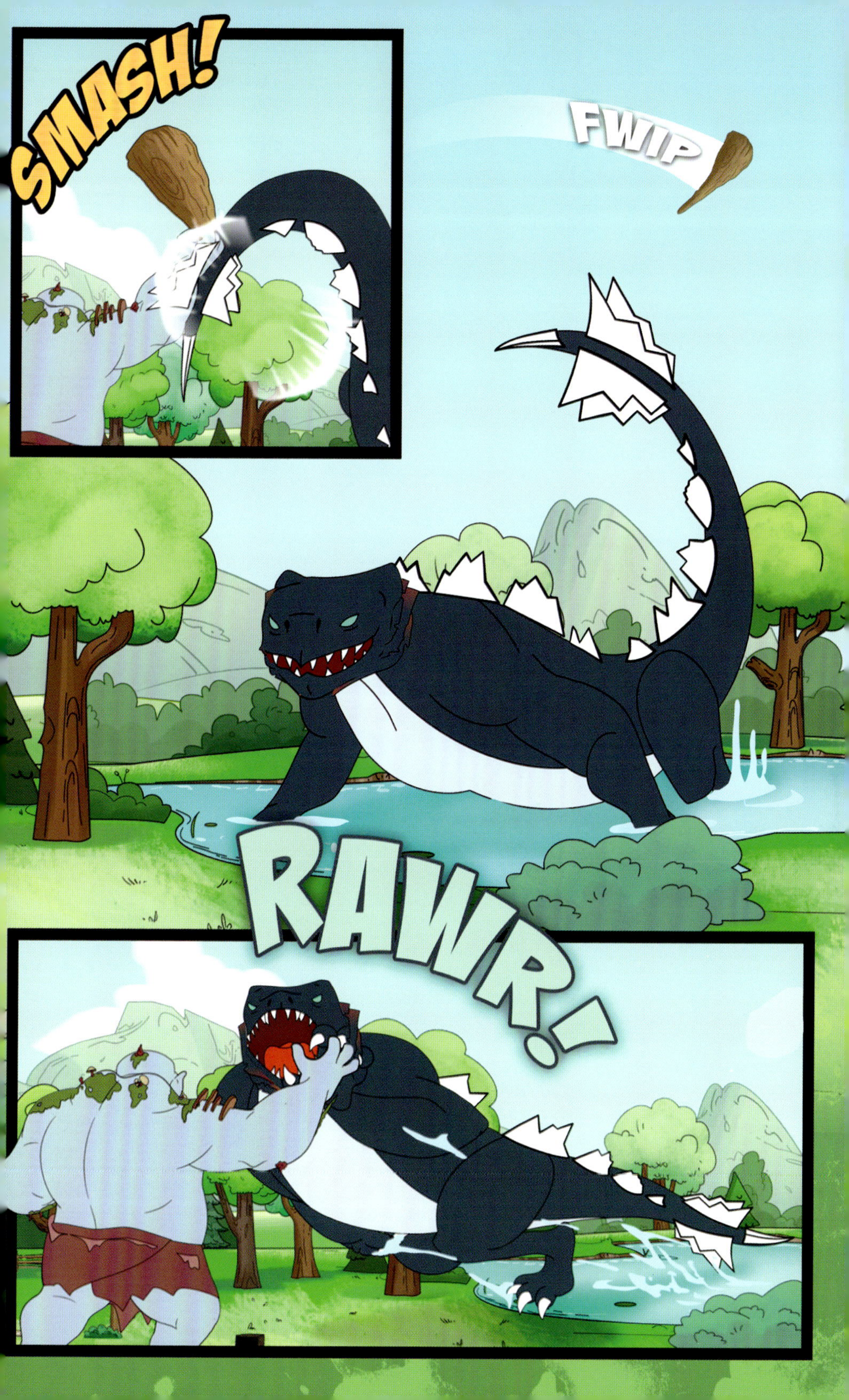
SMASH!
FWIP
RAWR!

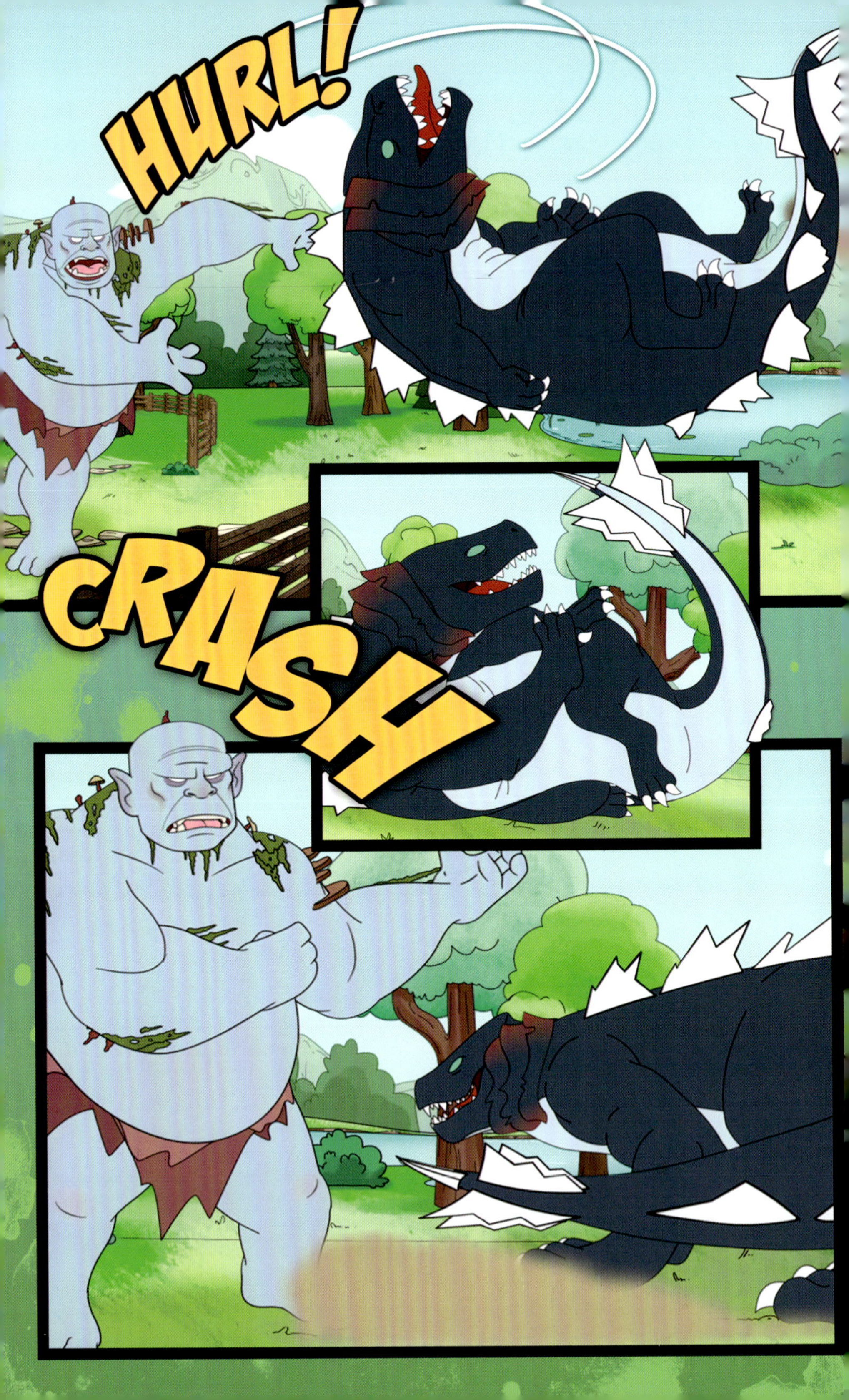
HURL!
CRASH

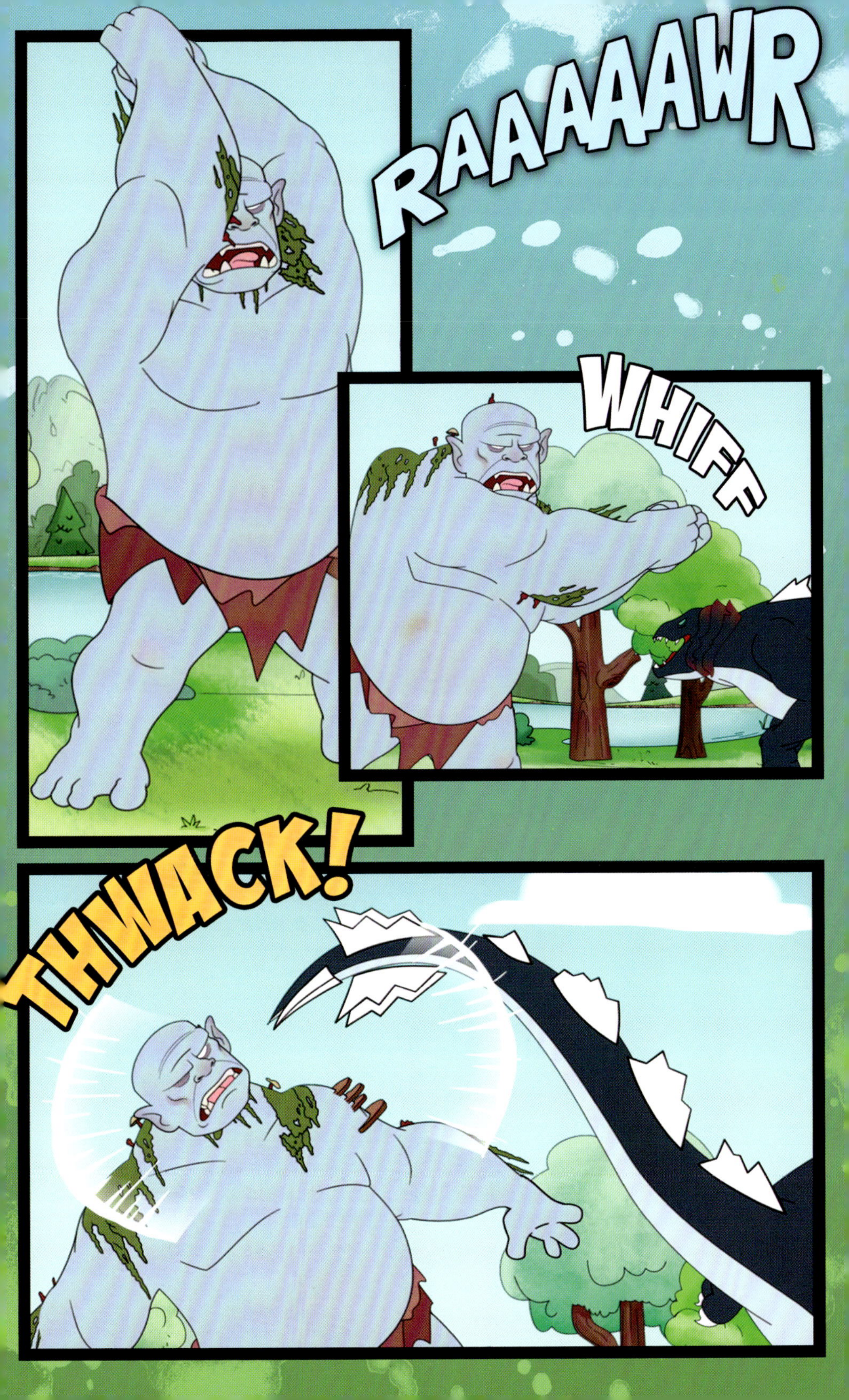
RAAAAAAWR
WHIFF
THWACK!

HRM?

RAAAAAWR

HEY, FROG-LADY! IT'S NOT WORKING!
HE JUST NEEDS MORE POWER!
SHEEPLE! GIVE THE LEVIATHAN YOUR POWER OR BE DESTROYED!
HMM...
OKAY!
HMM...

THAT'S NOT A GOOD IDEA.
WHEN YOU GROW A LEVIATHAN, IT ALMOST NEVER SHRINKS BACK DOWN!
BUT WE'RE SCAAAARED!
WE'LL GIVE YOU WHAT YOU WANT! JUST SAVE US!
SAVE US!
NO!
RIBBIT!
NO NO NO NO NO!

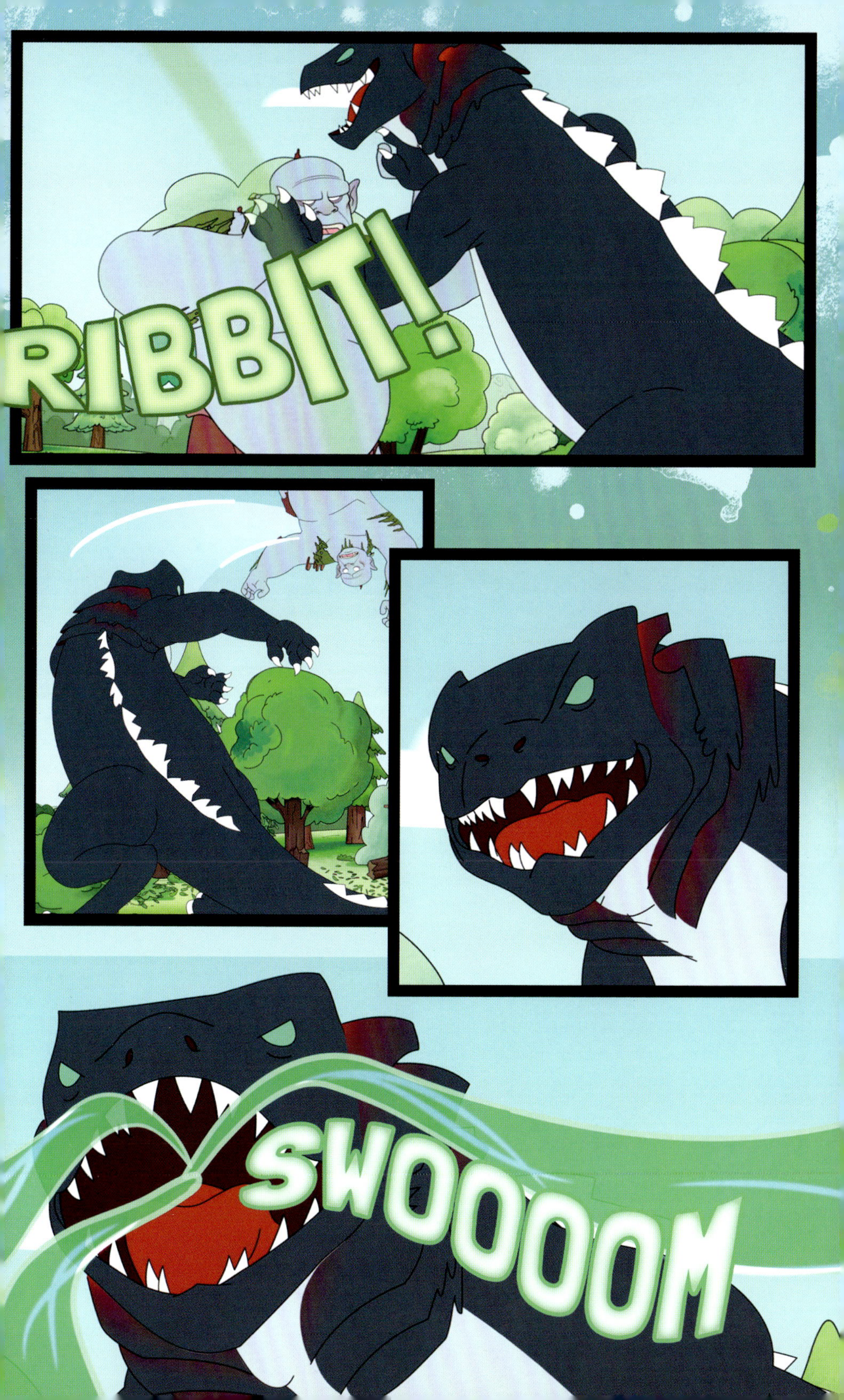
RIBBIT!
SWOOOOM

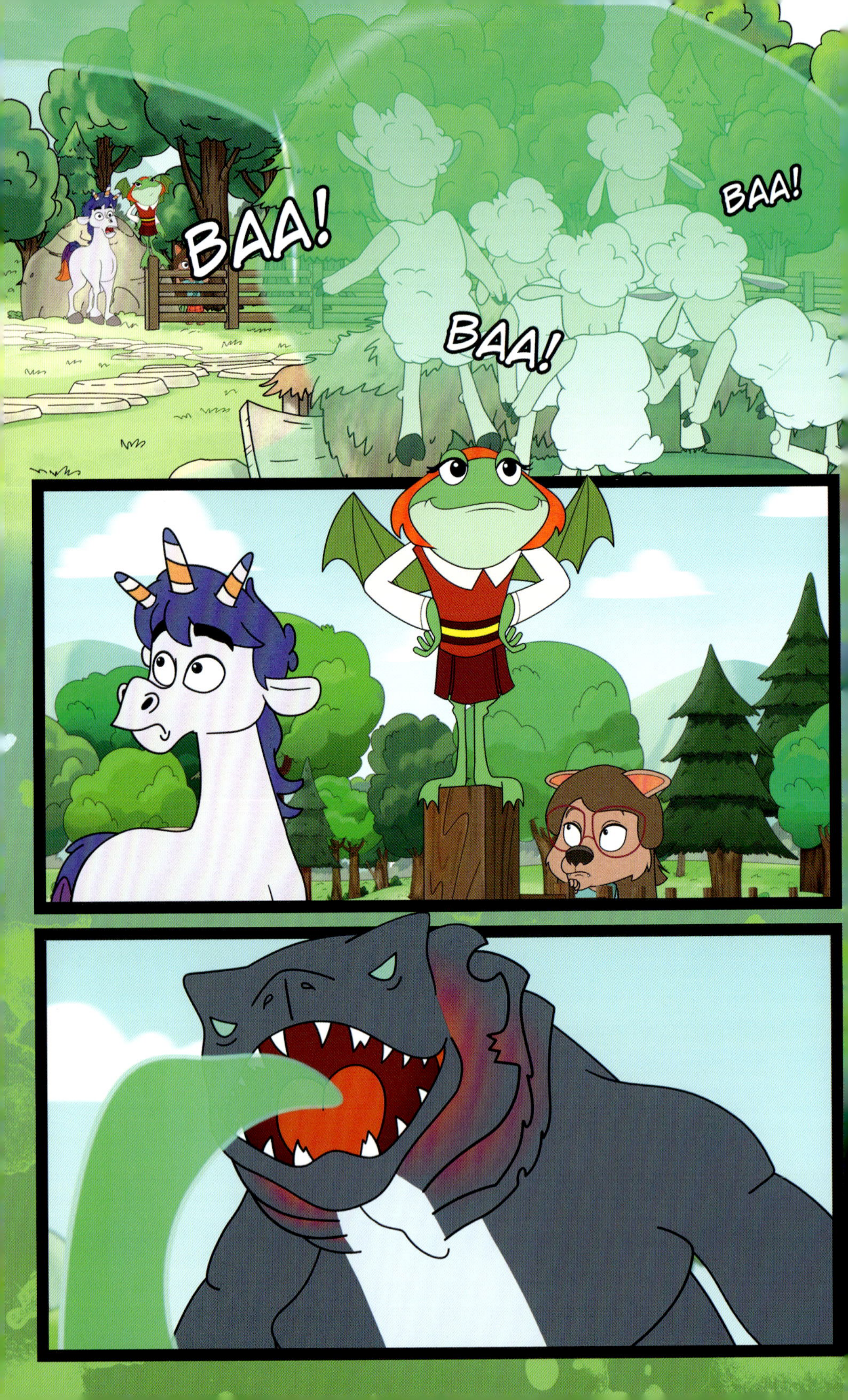
BAA!
BAA!
BAA!

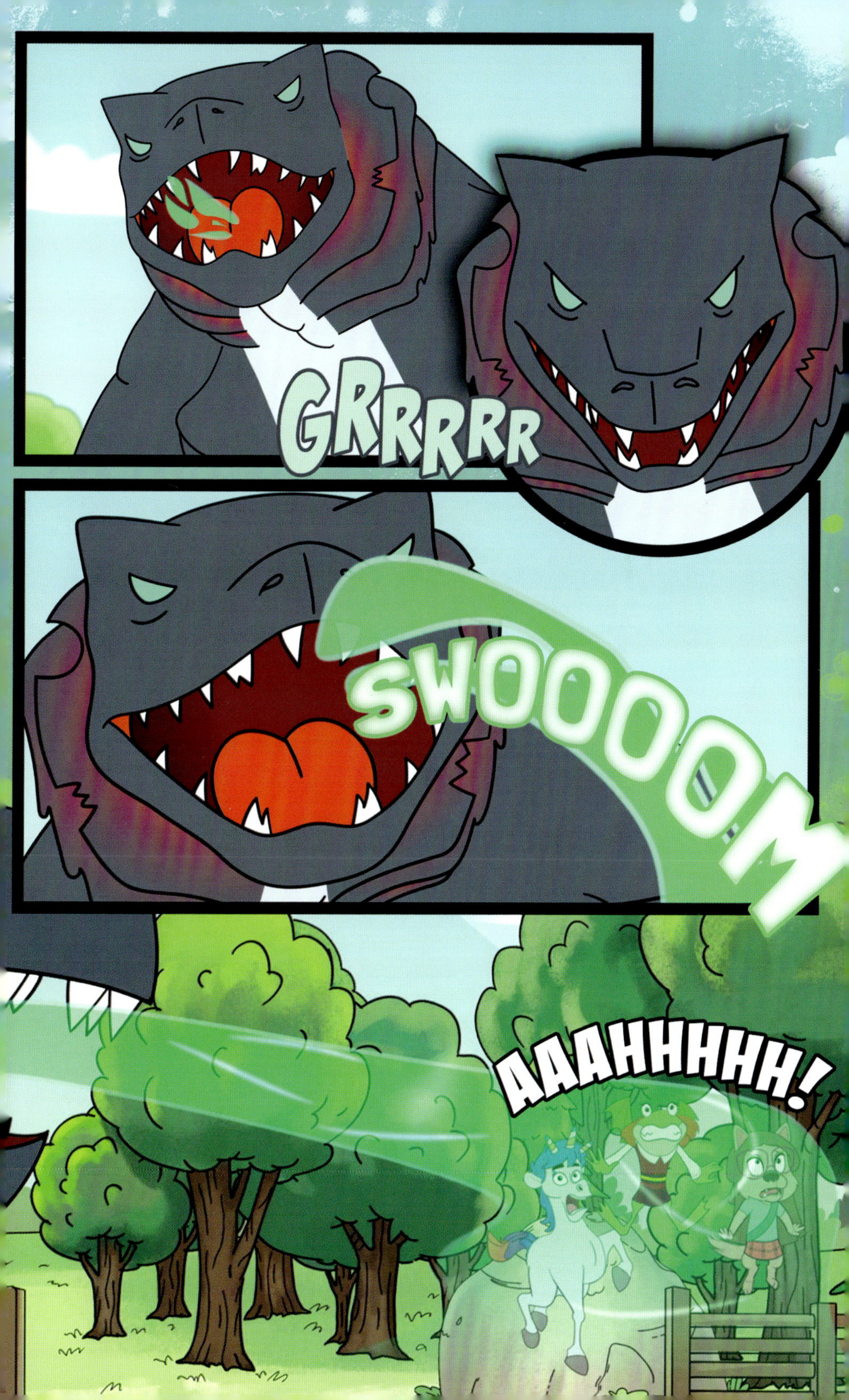
GRRRRRR
SWOOOOOM
AAAHHHHHH!

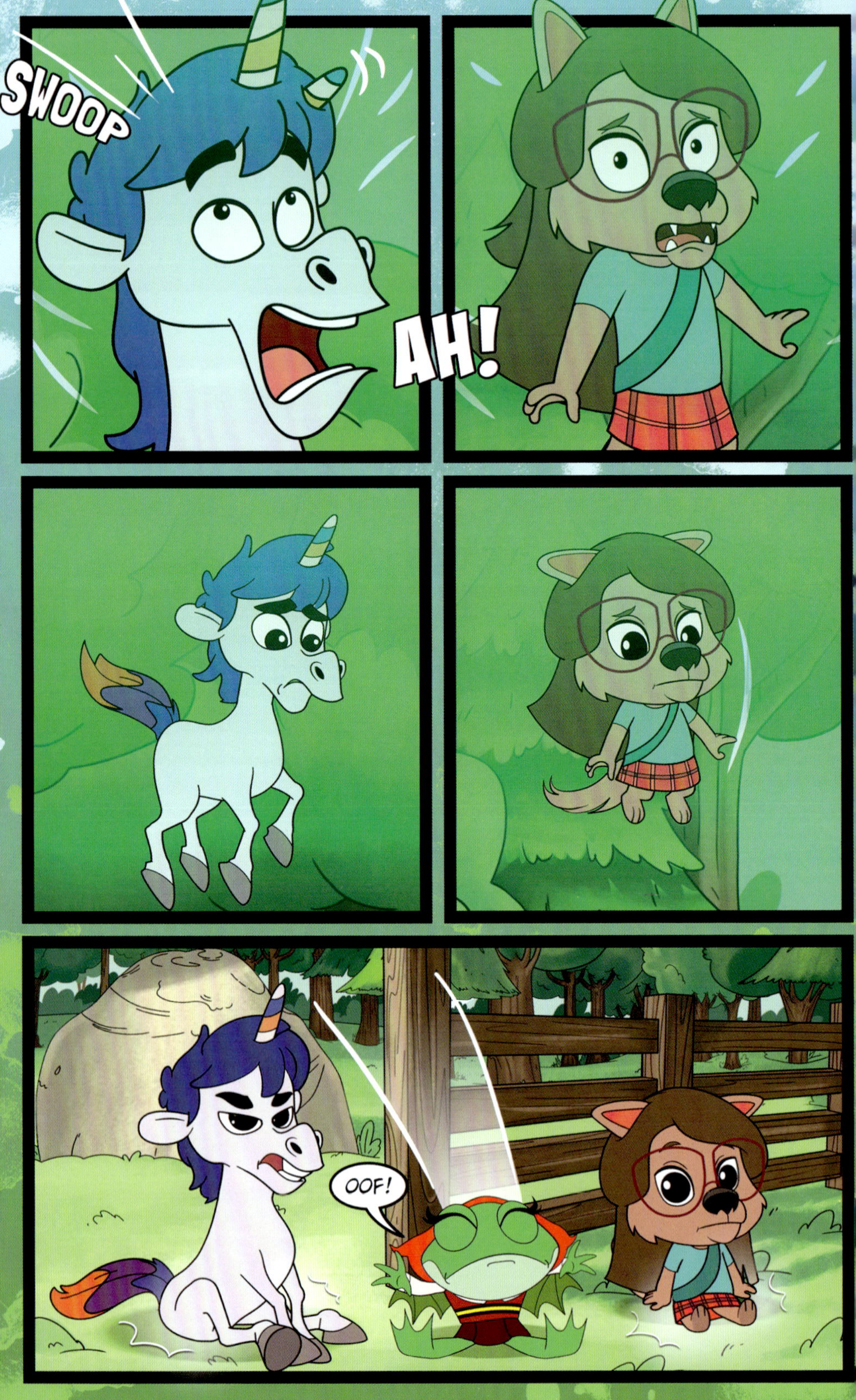
SWOOP
AH!
OOF!

WHAT HAVE YOU DONE?

GRrrrr

ROOOOAAAR!!!

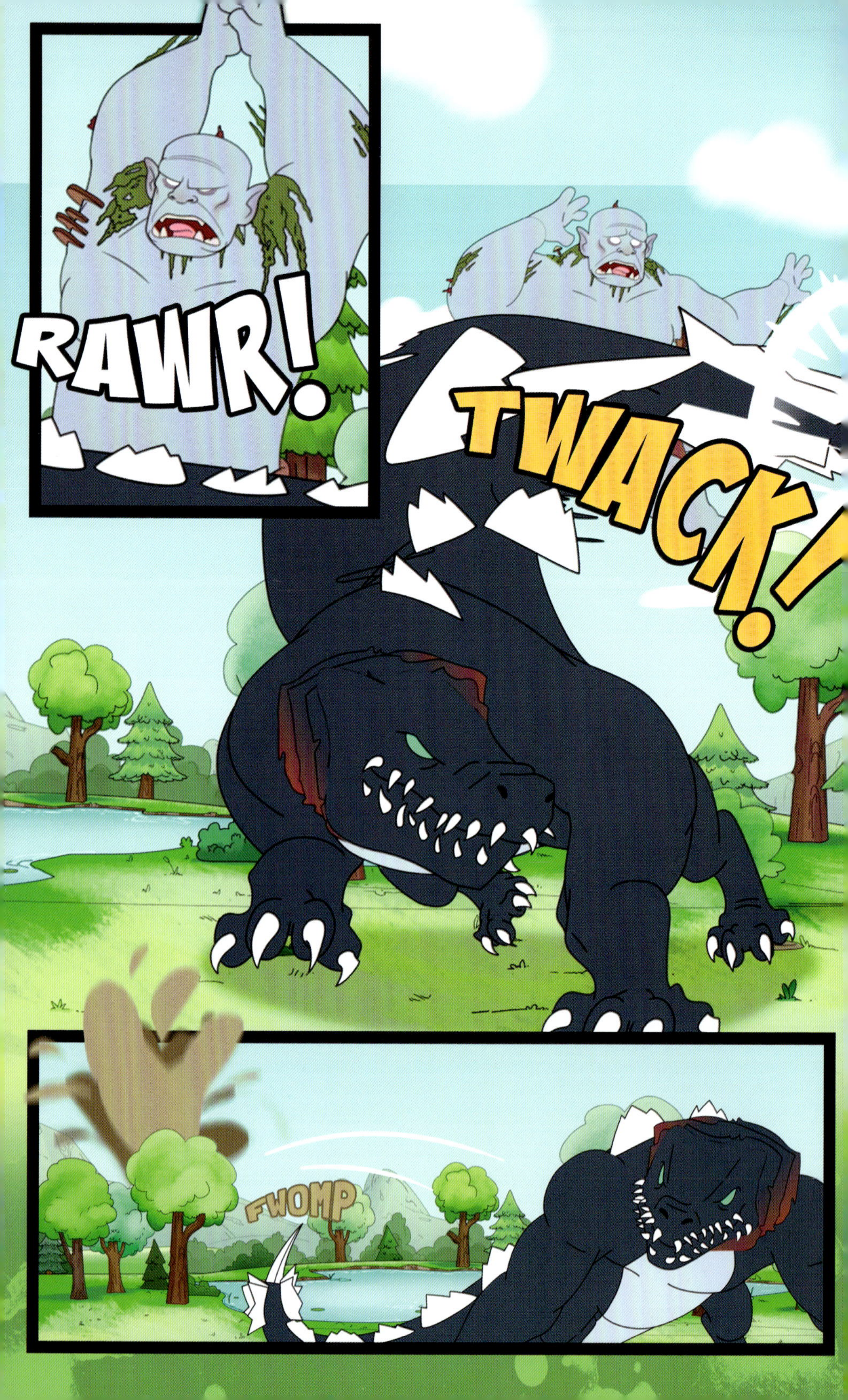
RAWR!
TWACK!
FWOMP

THE TERROR IS OVER!
YOU'RE WELCOME!
AND REMEMBER: GIVING POWER UP EVERY DAY KEEPS THE DANGER AWAY.
TWAP!
NOM
NOM

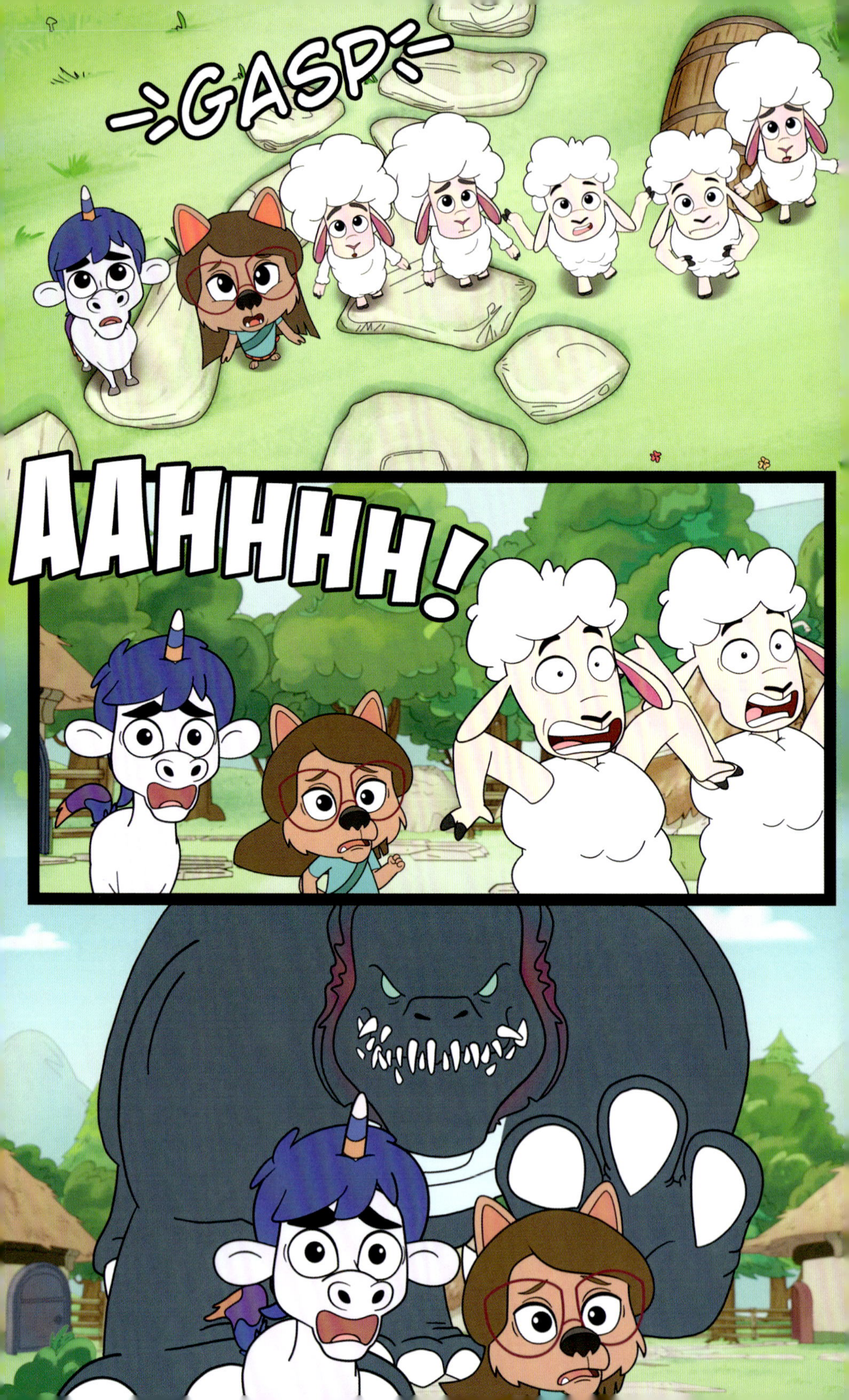
GASP
AAHHHH!

CLICK
CLICK

CRUNCH

WHAM!

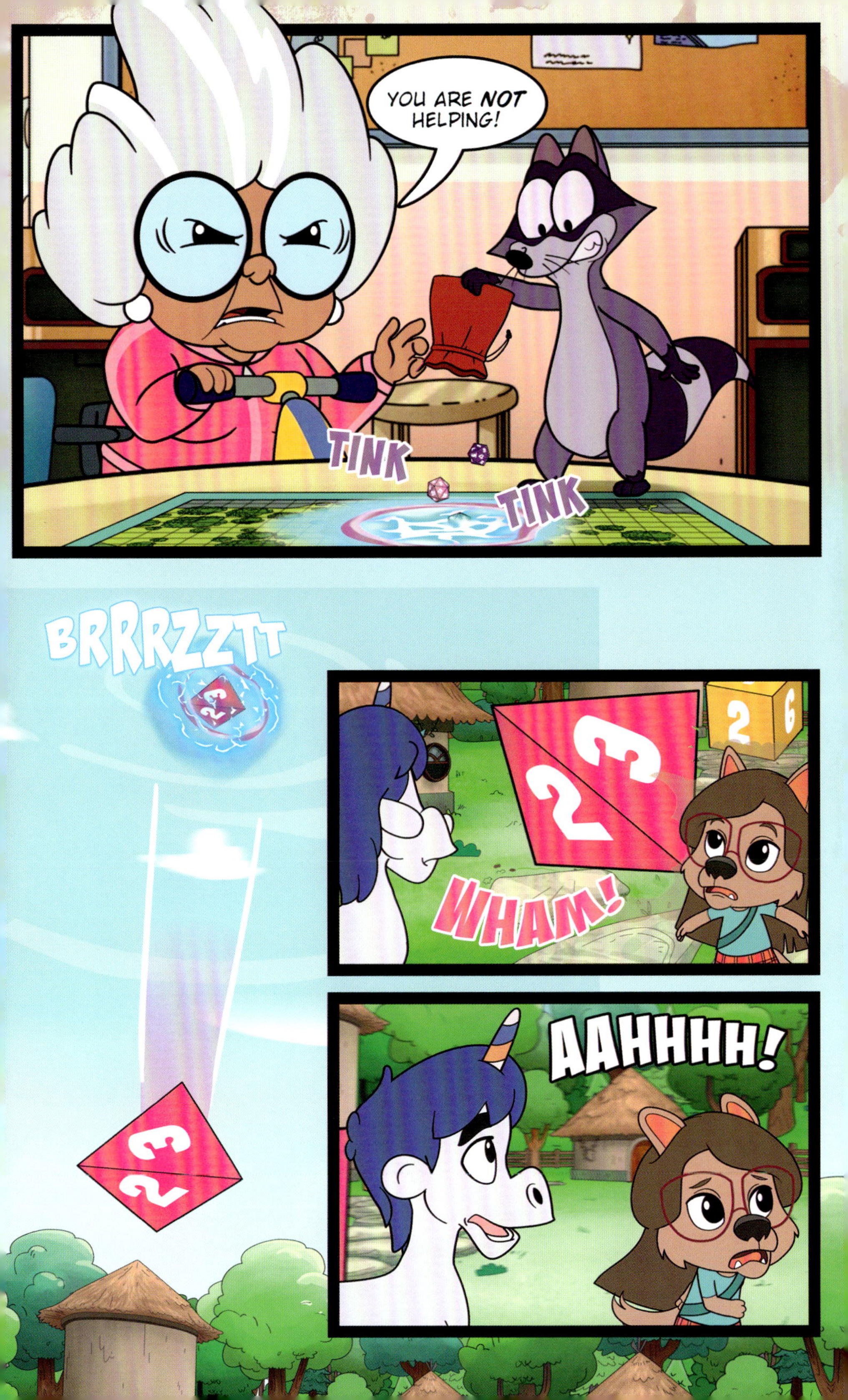

YOU ARE NOT HELPING!
TINK
TINK
BRRRZZTT
WHAM!
AAHHHH!

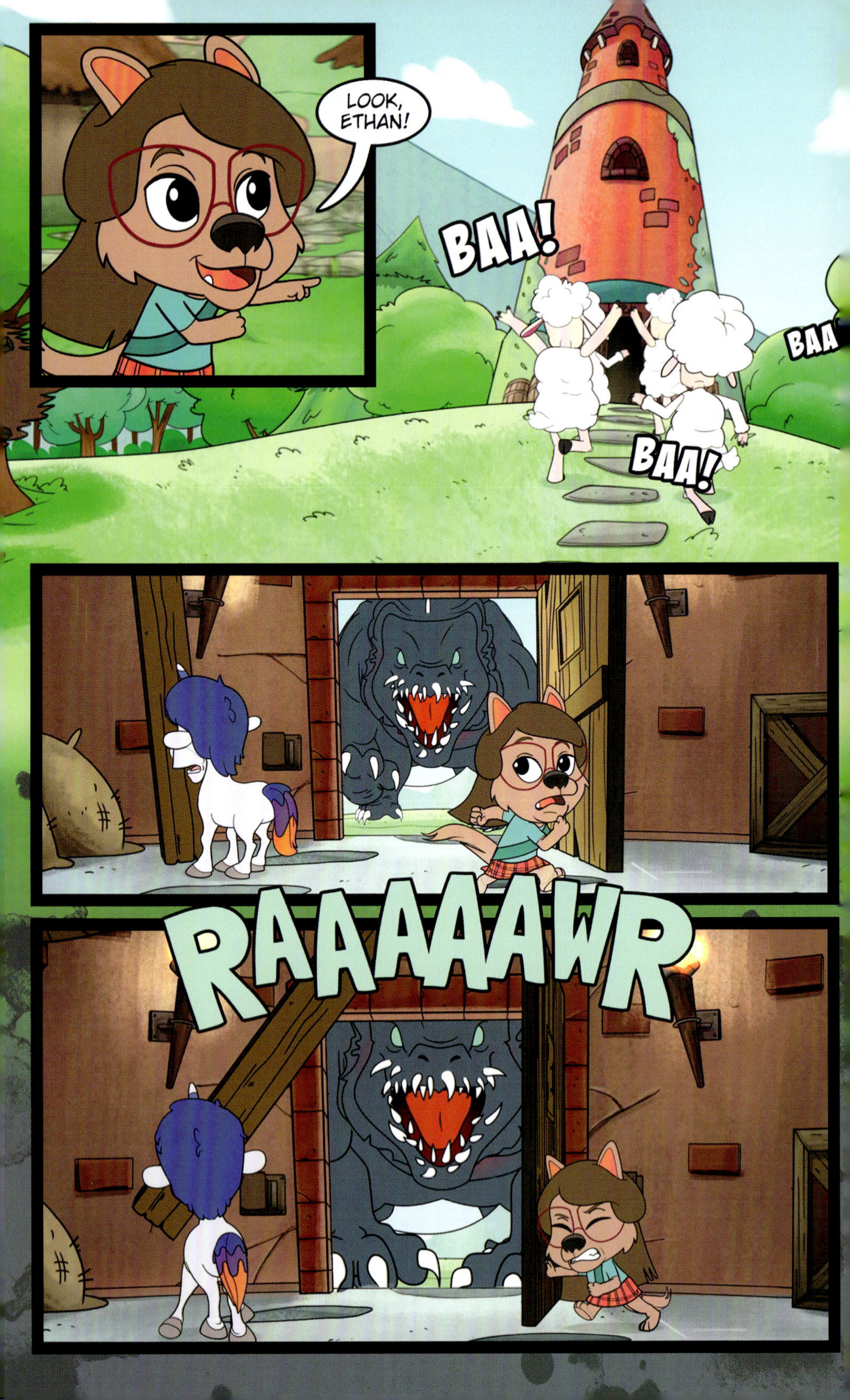
LOOK, ETHAN!
BAA!
BAA
BAA!
RAAAAAWR

BAM!
THINK, THINK! HOW DO WE STOP IT?
COOLIDGE SAID THAT IN A CRISIS, THE PEOPLE ARE THE BEST AT SOLVING THEIR OWN PROBLEMS.
BAM!
SO IF WE CAN EMPOWER THE VILLAGERS, MAYBE THEY CAN DEFEAT THE LEVIATHAN!
BAM!
IT'S WORTH A SHOT!
KNOCK
KNOCK
KNOCK
UH...

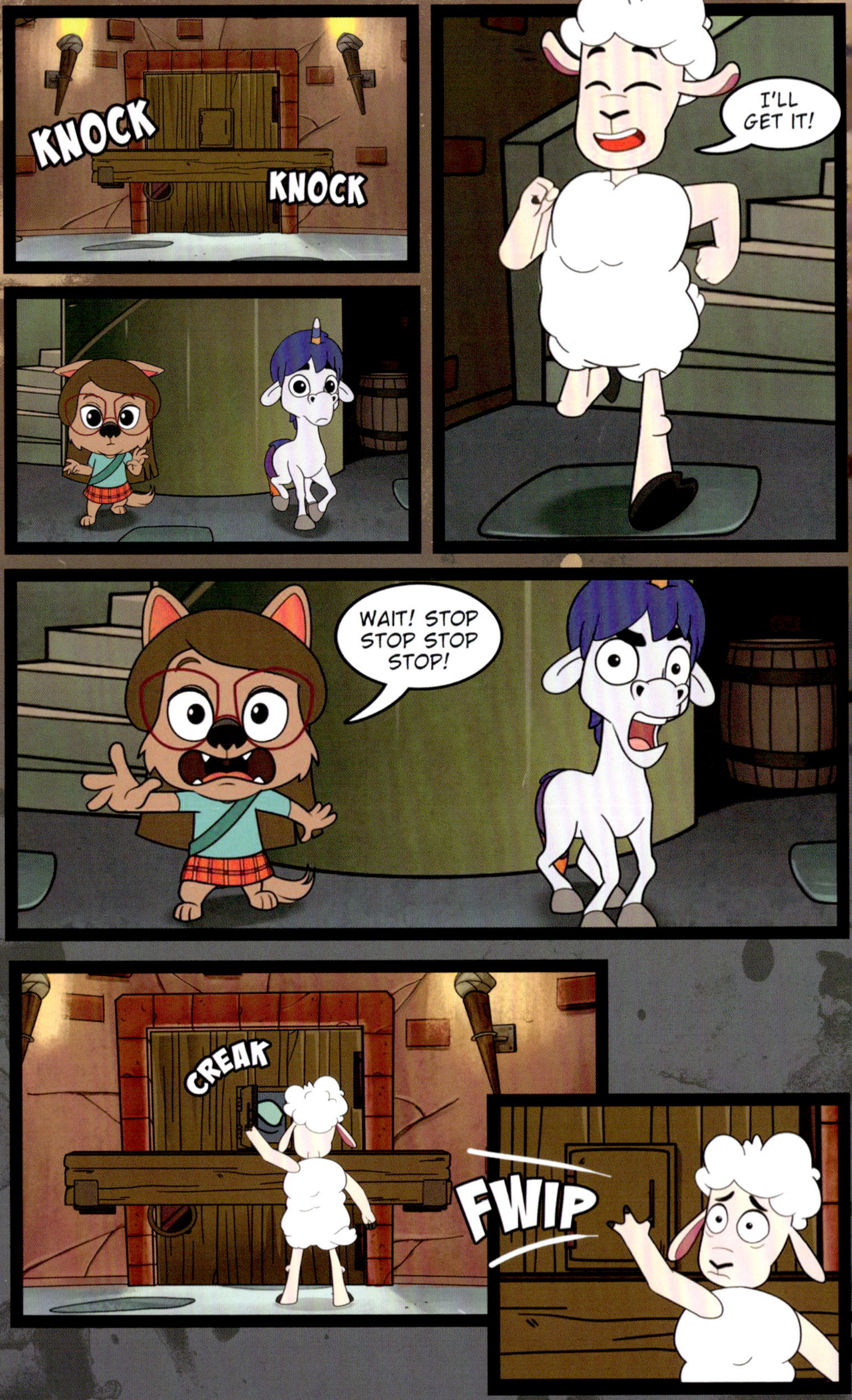
KNOCK
KNOCK
I'LL GET IT!
WAIT! STOP STOP STOP STOP!
CREAK
FWIP

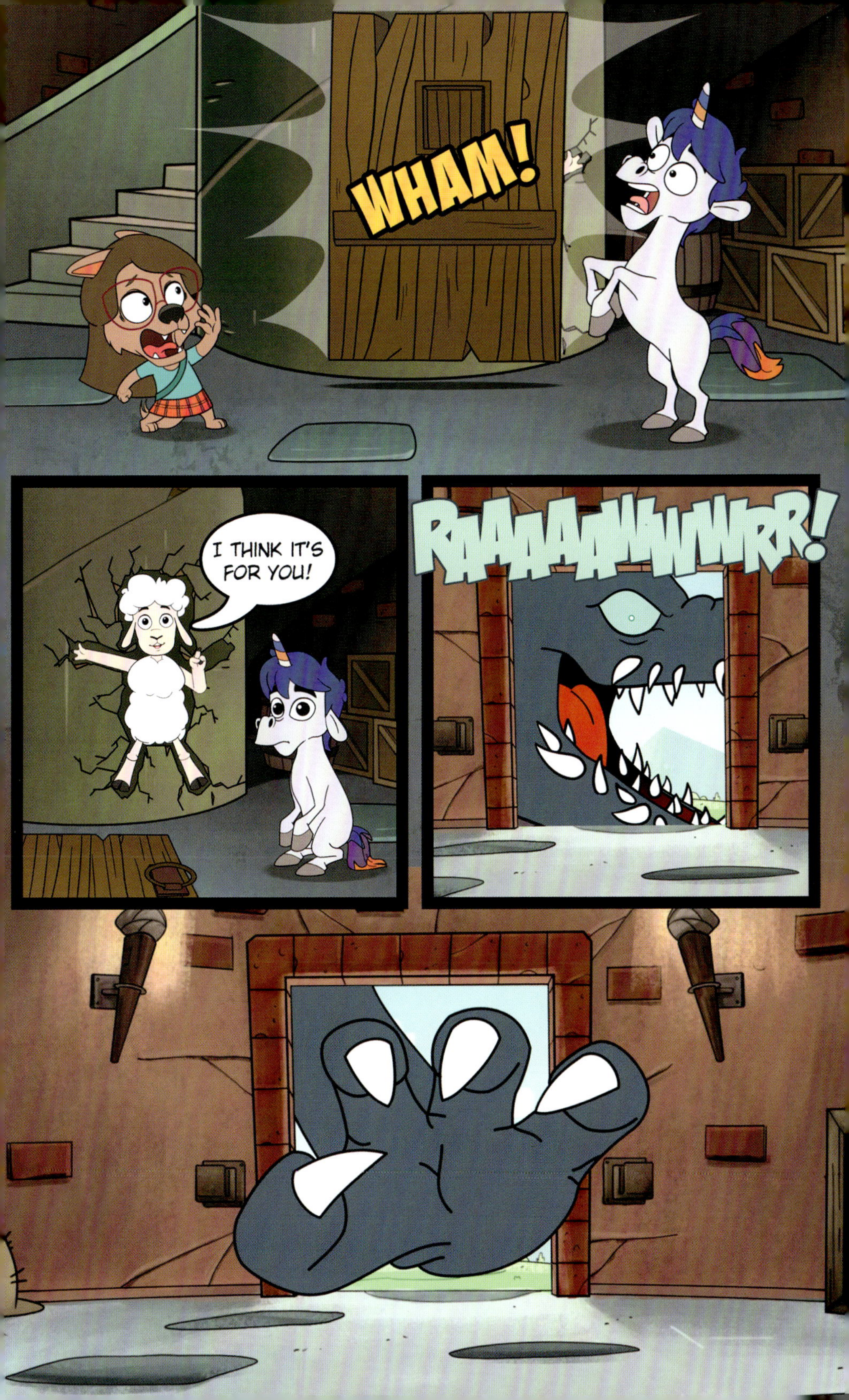
WHAM!
I THINK IT'S FOR YOU!
RAAAAAWWWRR!

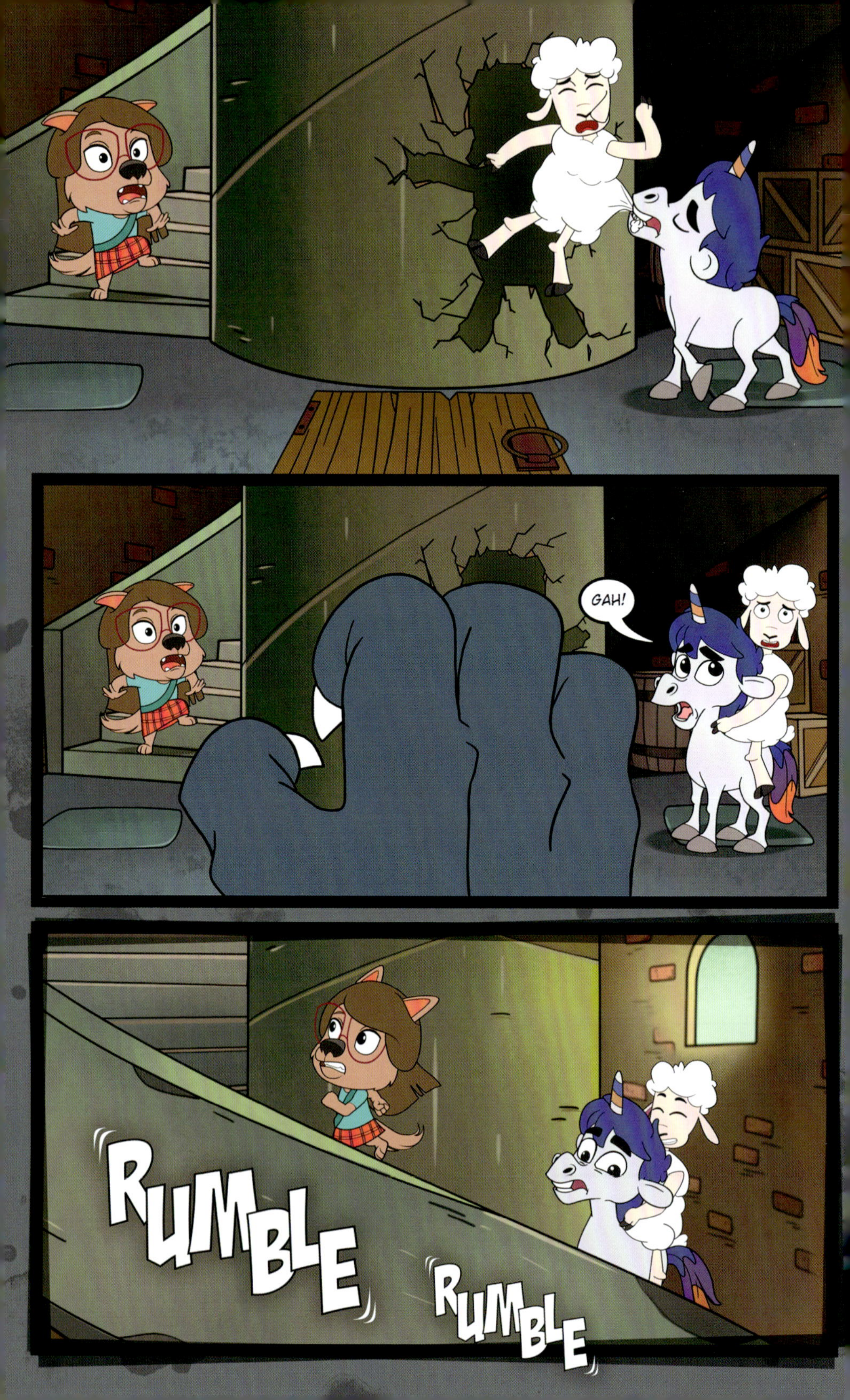
GAH!
RUMBLE
RUMBLE

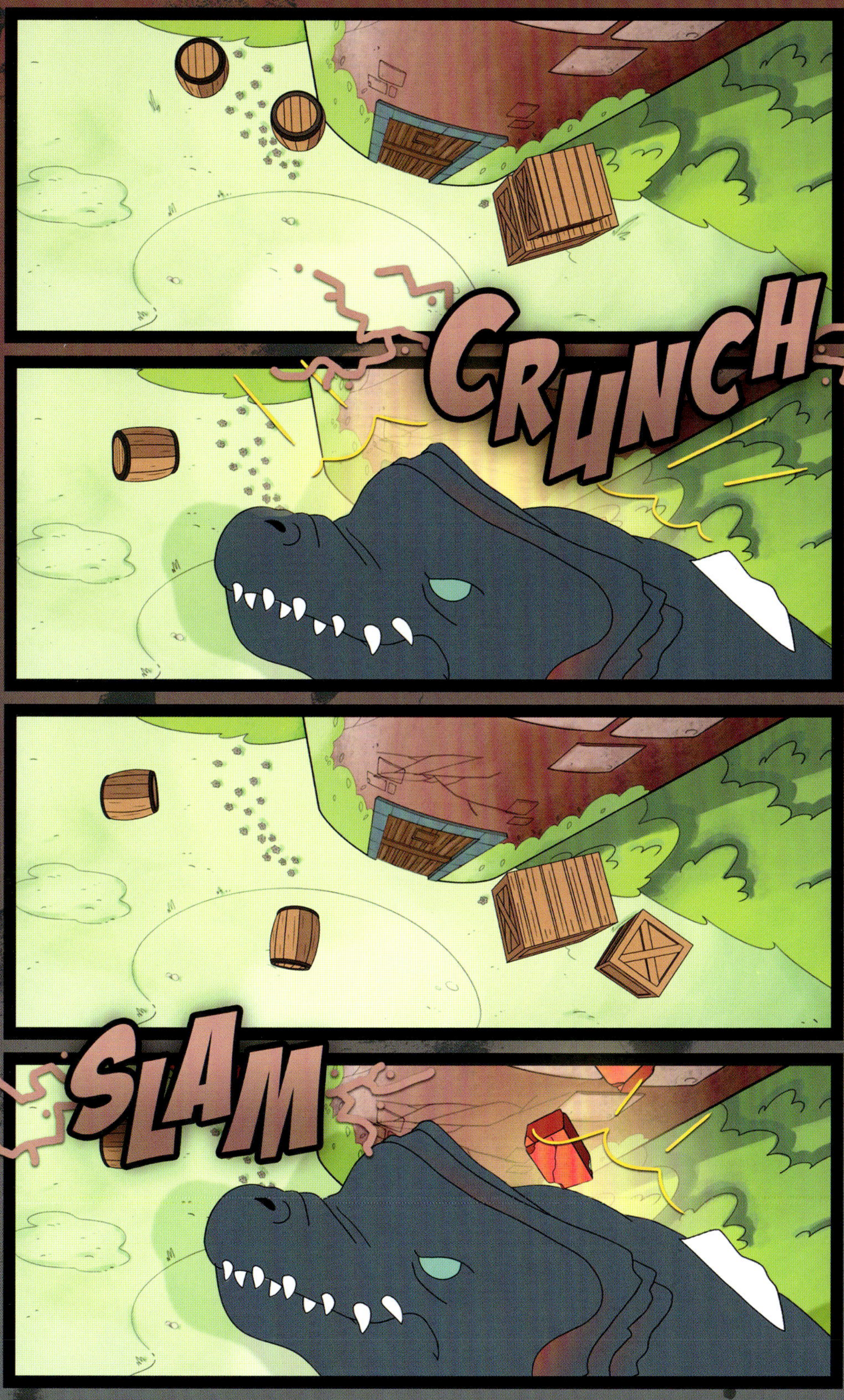
CRUNCH
SLAM

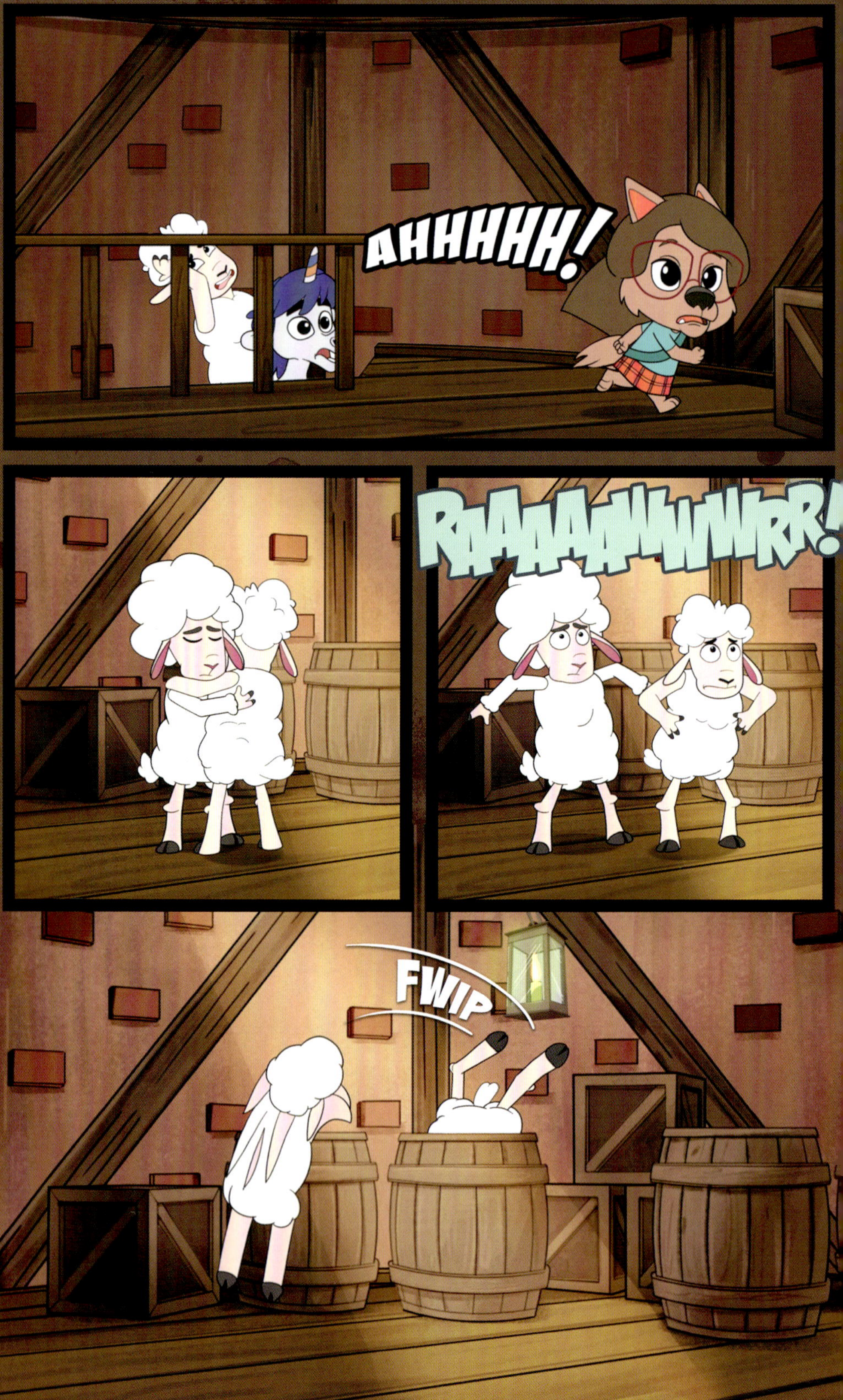
AHHHHH!
RAAAAAWWWRR!
FWIP

"EVERYONE... WITH A CRISIS, PEOPLE GIVE UP FREEDOMS BECAUSE THEY'RE **SCARED**..."

"...AND THAT MAKES THE GOVERNMENT POWER GROW BIGGER!"

BLOOP BLOOP

BRRRZZT

ZAP!

GASP!

ONCE A GOVERNMENT PROGRAM IS CREATED IT DOESN'T GO AWAY EASILY!
ZAP!
OOH, SO THIS IS WHAT PUBERTY'S LIKE!

THEY'RE RIGHT! WE HAVE THE POWER TO SOLVE OUR OWN PROBLEMS!
IT'S WORKING!!

BLOOP BLOOP BLOOP

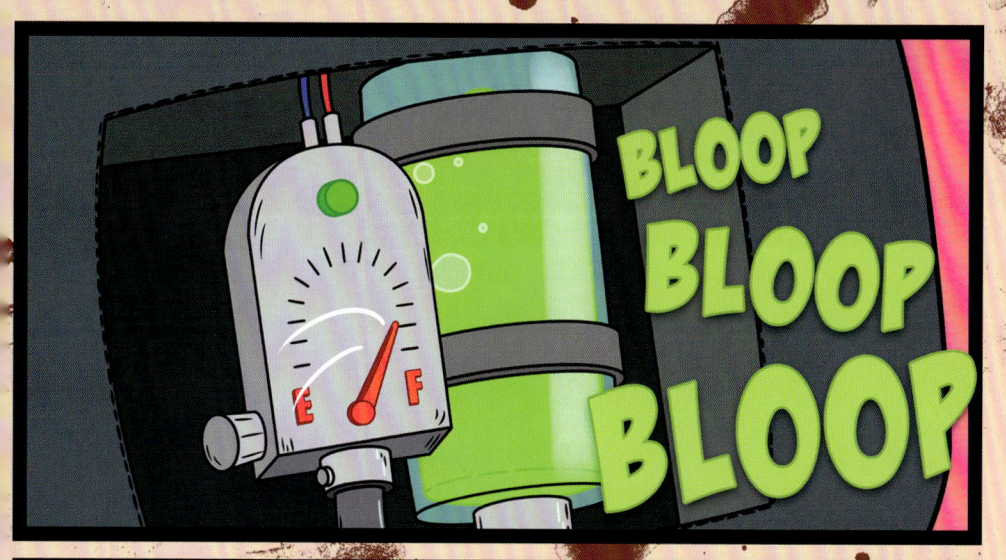

WOAH!

THE TRUTH MADE US *JACKED!*

YEAH! I UPGRADED TO A *QUADRICORN!*

SHEEPLE!

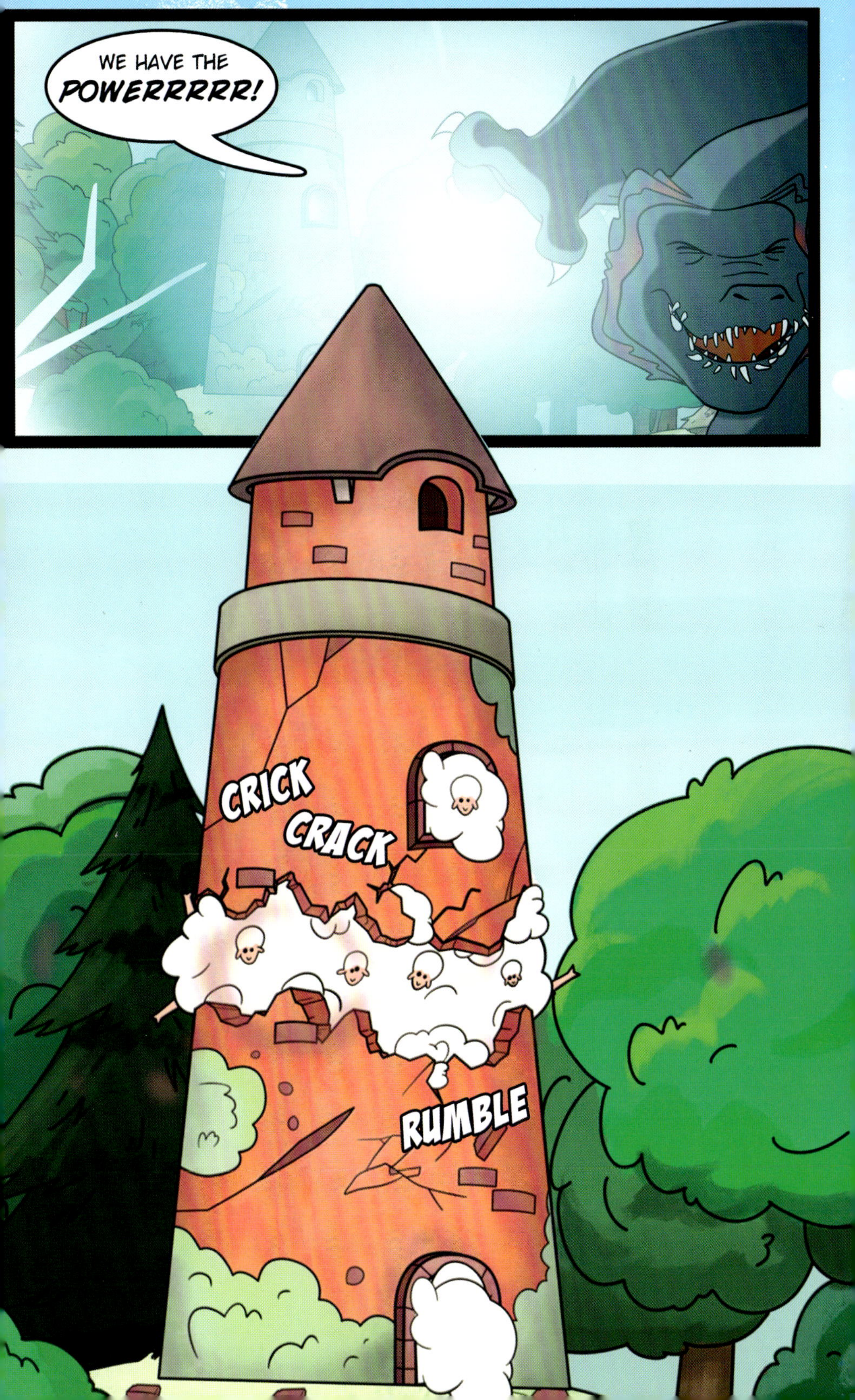
WE HAVE THE POWERRRRR!
CRICK
CRACK
RUMBLE

BRAAA... WWW!

GRRRRR

BAAAAAAAAA!

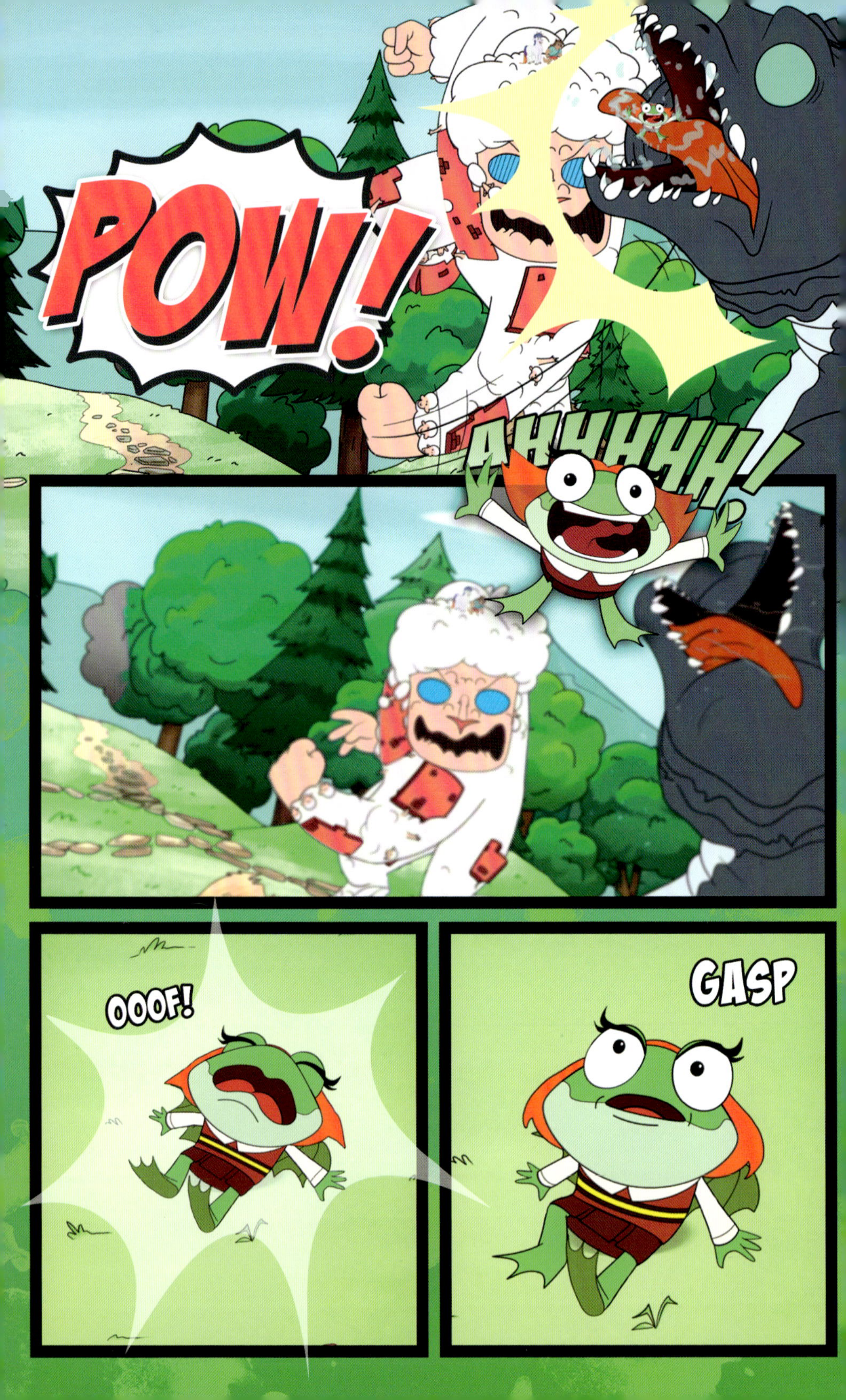
POW!
AHHHHH!
OOOF!
GASP

BAM!

CRASH!

ROOOOAAAR!

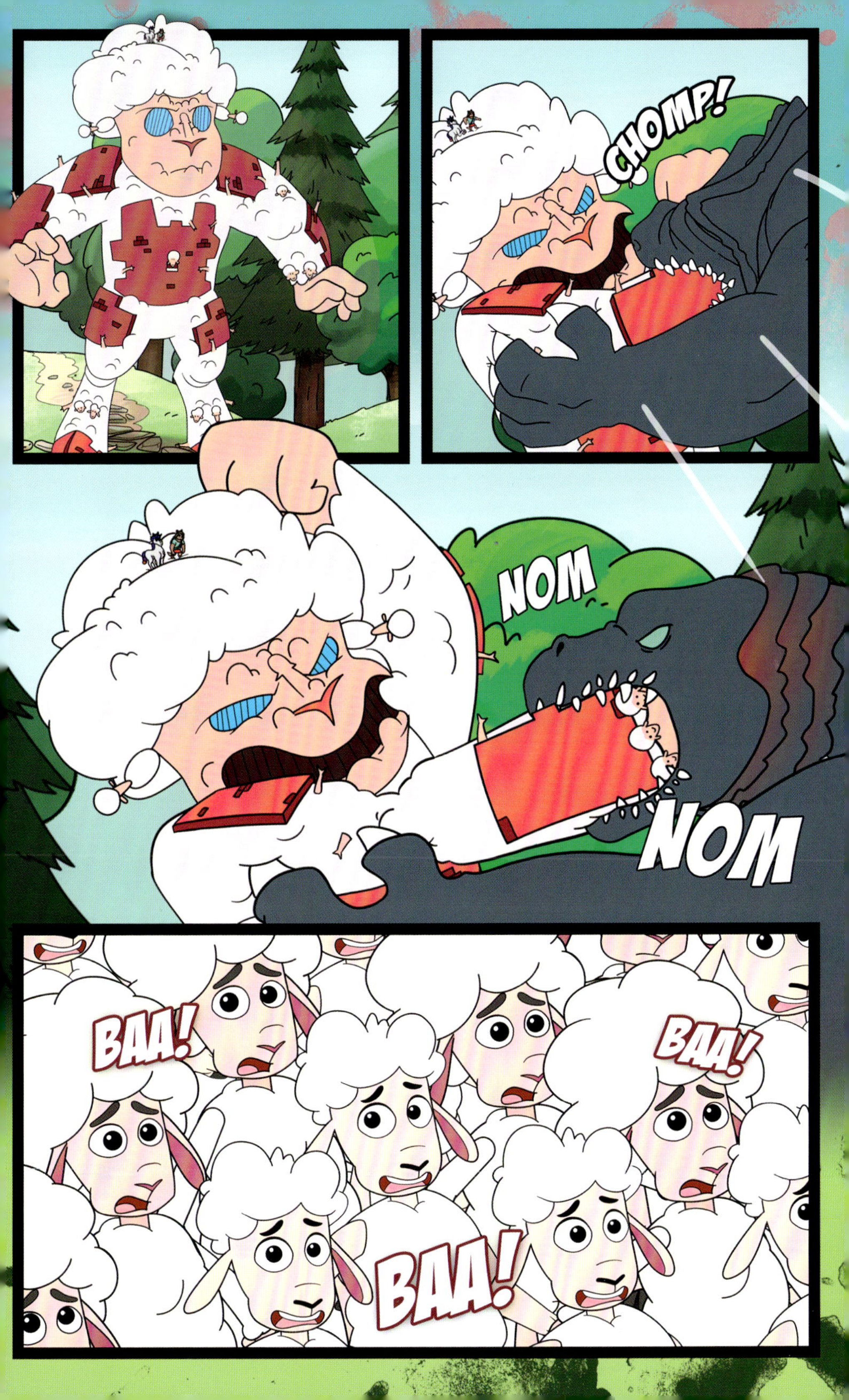
CHOMP!
NOM
NOM
BAA!
BAA!
BAA!

DON'T GIVE INTO FEAR!!

YOU CAN TAKE BACK YOUR POWER!

SQUEAK!

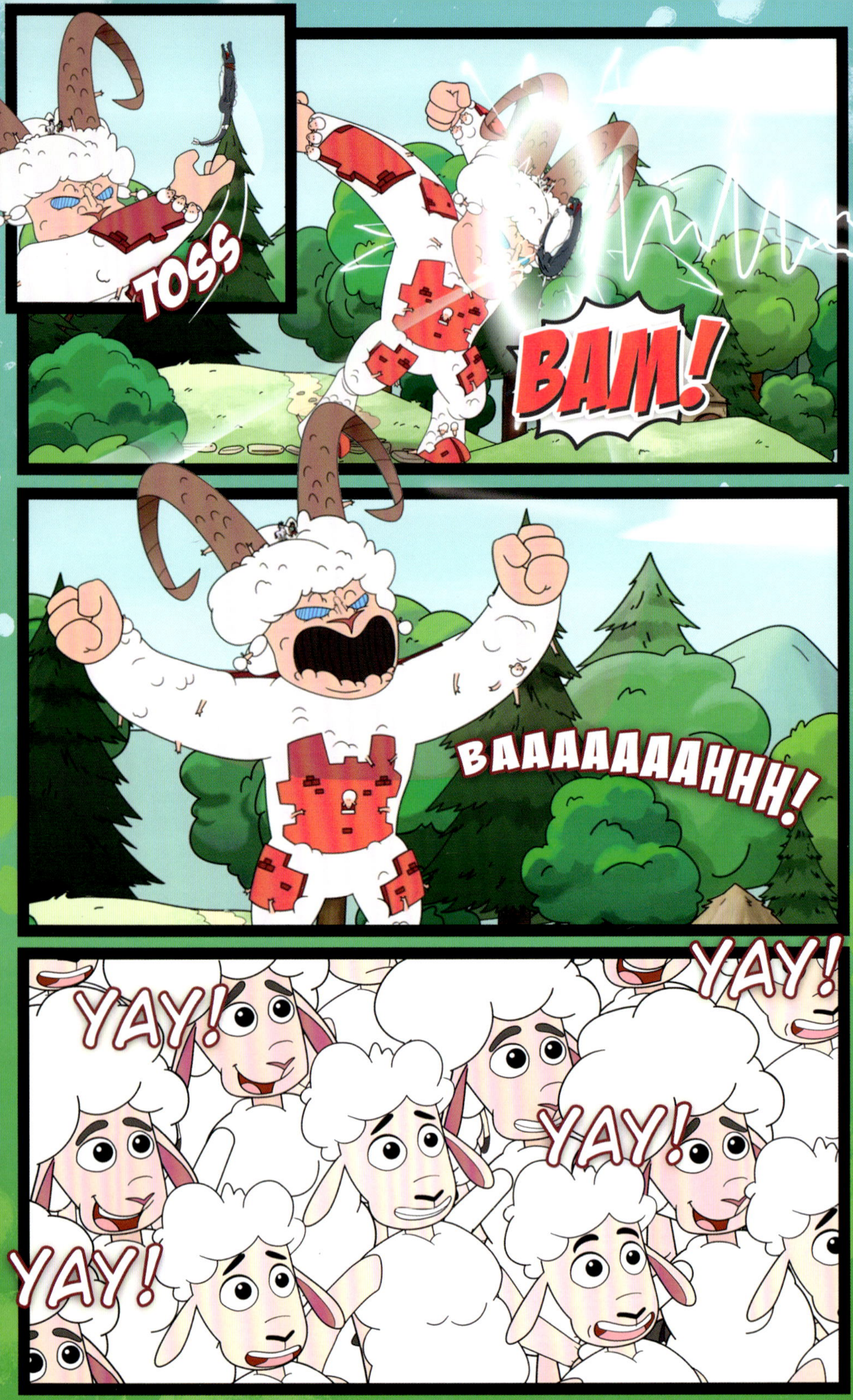
TOSS
BAM!
BAAAAAAAAHHH!
YAY!
YAY!
YAY!
YAY!

YOU DID IT!
YOU SOLVED THE PROBLEM YOURSELVES!
BLOOP
BLOOP
BLOOP
E
F
SHEEPLE! SHEEPLE!
BRRRZZTT

OW!
WE DID IT!! OH, I'VE NEVER BEEN SO HAPPY TO BE BACK IN MY OWN BODY!
I'M NOT!
SEE!? BACK TO REGULAR DANDRUFF...

THERE'S NO TIME TO MOPE ABOUT YOUR DANDRUFF, ETHAN!
5:30PM
LOOK AT THE WRIST WATCH ON MY BEAUTIFUL HUMAN WRIST!
THE CITY COUNCIL MEETING- IT'S ABOUT TO START!
HEY, YOU LOOK LIKE YOU'RE GOING SOMEWHERE IMPORTANT. WANT A RIDE?

CITY HALL
AND THAT'S WHY I CAN'T STAND FOR THIS NEW DEPARTMENT!
OH, COME ON, PEOPLE!
IT'S SIMPLE: EITHER THE GOVERNMENT SWOOPS IN AND GIVES US MONEY TO PAY OUR EMPLOYEES, OR WE HAVE TO START FIRING PEOPLE.

THAT'S WHY THE COUNCIL SHOULD APPOINT ME AS THE HEAD OF THE ECONOMIC STIMULUS DEPARTMENT, AND I WILL MAKE SURE YOU GET ALL THE MONEY YOU NEED.

WE CAN'T DO THIS ALONE.

WITHOUT THE GOVERNMENT, WE'RE POWERLESS.

THAT OVERLY-DRESSED MAN COULDN'T BE MORE WRONG!

WE'RE ONLY POWERLESS IF WE GIVE OUR POWER AWAY!

BUT WE'RE SCARED! IF THE GOVERNMENT DOESN'T HELP US THROUGH THIS CRISIS, WHO WILL?

NO ONE. YOU'LL DIE ALONE!
WE'LL HELP EACH OTHER!
WE, AS A COMMUNITY, ARE SO MUCH BETTER AT SOLVING OUR OWN PROBLEMS THAN THE GOVERNMENT EVER COULD BE.
COUGH
COUGH
YES, EXACTLY! MR. JASPERSON! HOW LONG DID IT TAKE THE ROAD REPAIR DEPARTMENT TO FIX THAT POTHOLE IN FRONT OF YOUR BUSINESS?
IT TOOK EIGHT MONTHS. I SHOULD'VE JUST HAD THE SCOUTS HELP ME FIX IT.

AND, MS. HIGGINS, WHEN TAXES WERE RAISED TO HELP YOUR SCHOOL, DID YOUR CLASSROOM SEE ANY OF THAT MONEY?
WELL, NO... BUT LUCKILY MY CHURCH DID A SCHOOL SUPPLY DRIVE TO MAKE SURE MY CLASS HAD EVERYTHING THEY NEEDED.
AND, OLD MAN CHUCKFREY, WAS IT THE GOVERNMENT WHO REMOVED THOSE BEES FROM YOUR ATTIC?
THEY WANTED TO, BUT THEM BEES IS FAMILY!
THAT'S A BAD EXAMPLE, BUT THE POINT IS:

IT'S NOT THE GOVERNMENT WHO WILL SAVE YOU IN A CRISIS, IT'S THE PEOPLE AROUND YOU.

BUT THEIR HELP MIGHT NOT MEET APPROVED STANDARDS.

MAYBE NOT. AND CRISI- C-CRISES- W- WHATEVER.

THEY'RE HARD, BUT GIVING OUR POWER TO AN EVER- GROWING GOVERNMENT ONLY MAKES THINGS HARDER.

AND GIVING INTO FEAR MAKES YOUR POWER DISAPPEAR.

SOMETIMES, THE MEDICINE IS WORSE THAN THE DISEASE.

PAT
PAT
AND SOMETIMES THE MEDICINE IS YUMMY!
SAY IT WITH ME "THE MEDICINE IS YUMMY!"
VOTE YES ON PROPOSITION 20!

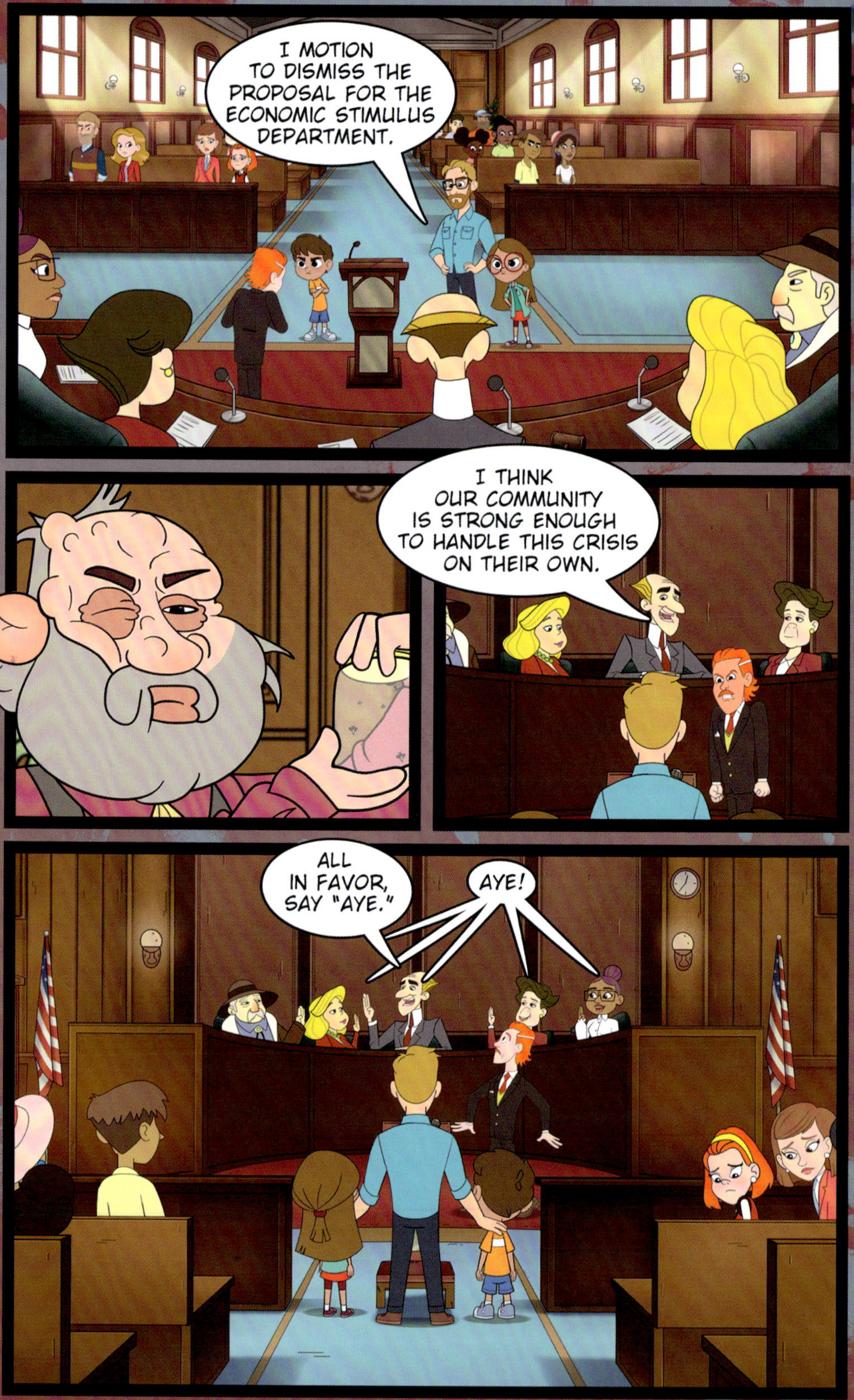
I MOTION TO DISMISS THE PROPOSAL FOR THE ECONOMIC STIMULUS DEPARTMENT.
I THINK OUR COMMUNITY IS STRONG ENOUGH TO HANDLE THIS CRISIS ON THEIR OWN.
ALL IN FAVOR, SAY "AYE."
AYE!

THE COUNCIL HAS REJECTED THE STIMULUS.

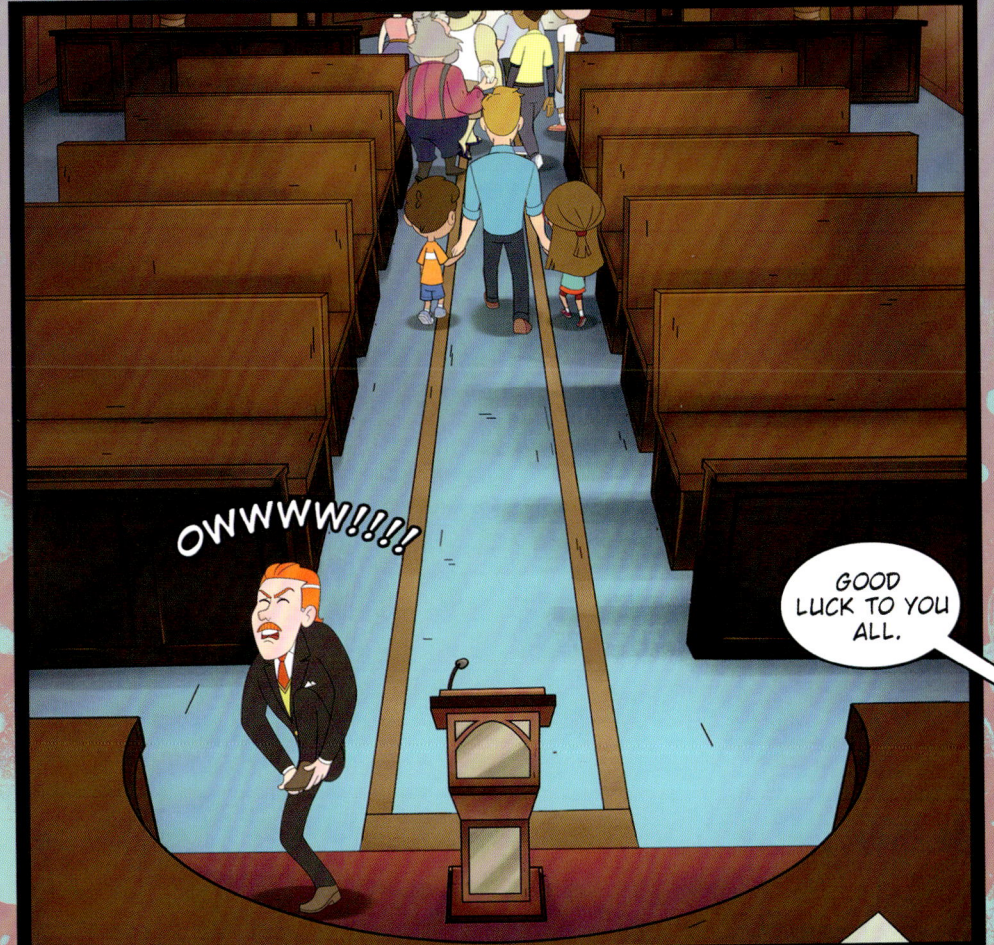

WHAT!?

WHACK!

OWWWW!!!!

GOOD LUCK TO YOU ALL.

YOU TWO WERE AMAZING IN THERE. I COULDN'T BE MORE PROUD.
THANKS, DAD. I KNOW THAT IF WE WORK TOGETHER WE CAN HELP TRINA KEEP HER JOB AS A BARISTA AND AS THE BEST C&C GAME MASTER IN TOWN.
BEST C&C GAME MASTER...
The Idea
ETHAN! THAT GIVES ME AN IDEA.

YOU APPROACH THE HOARD OF GOLD AND IT GLISTENS IN THE MOONLIGHT.
SUDDENLY, A GIANT TROLL SPRINGS UP FROM THE GOLD!
ROLL FOR INITIATIVE.
AWESOME!!
BZZT
BEEP BEEP
WELL, I GOTTA GET GOING GUYS.

WELL, ACTUALLY, TRINA, WOULD YOU BE WILLING TO GO BACK TO YOUR NORMAL HOURS?

YES, I WOULD LOVE TO! BUT HOW WILL YOU AFFORD IT? DID WE GET THAT GOVERNMENT MONEY?

ACTUALLY, WE DIDN'T NEED IT. WE USED OUR OWN POWERS.

WHAT IS THIS?

YES!

I THINK WE CAN HANDLE THAT.

PEPPER SPRAAAAYYY!

NOT INSIDE, COPERNICUS!